This book was originally published as *Iedereen kan leiden*, LannooCampus, 2021.

D/2021/45/518 – ISBN 978 94 014 8196 0 – NUR 800, 808

Cover and interior design: Gert Degrande | De Witlofcompagnie
Translation: Ian Connerty

LannooCampus Publishers is a subsidiary of Lannoo Publishers,
the book and multimedia division of Lannoo Publishers nv.

LannooCampus Publishers
Vaartkom 41 box 01.02
3000 Leuven
Belgium
www.lannoocampus.com

P.O. Box 23202
1100 DS Amsterdam
Netherlands

Everyone Can Lead

Frans van de Ven | *Personal Leadership in Organisations*

Lannoo
Campus

▶ *Contents*

ENSŌ

The symbol on the cover of this book is an *ensō*. Ensō is the Japanese word for 'circle'. Drawing the ensō symbol by hand is regarded as an important meditation exercise in Zen Buddhism, during which the mind is fully in the moment.

According to Audrey Yoshiko Seo, author of *Ensō: Zen Circles of Enlightenment*, ensō 'are symbols of (amongst other things) personal development, reality and enlightenment. Seemingly perfect in their continuity, balance and feeling of completeness and yet often irregular in their execution, ensō are simultaneously the most simple and the most complex form. They seem to allow little room for variation, but in the hands of Zen masters the range of personal expressions they can convey is almost limitless.'

Ensō perfectly represents the things for which this book and my vision on leadership stand. It is a practical handbook, based on everyday reality. Not a lifeless summary of regurgitated methodology, but a guide that can lead you towards the development of your own form of leadership. A digest of fundamentally simple principles that you can apply in your own unique and authentic way.

The ensō circle can be closed or open, as shown on the cover of this book. An open circle is incomplete, so that further movement and development is possible. Zen practitioners relate the idea of the open circle to the concept of *wabi-sabi*, a view of the world focused on the acceptance of transience and imperfection. The seven dimensions of wabi-sabi are: *fukinsei* (asymmetry and imperfection), *kanso* (simplicity), *koko* (soberness), *shizen* (naturalness), *yugen* (subtlety), *datsuzoku* (freedom) and *seijaku* (tranquillity). These principles can all be found in nature, but also in human character and behaviour. Wabi-sabi underlines the importance of re-establishing contact with these principles. And that is precisely what we will also do by applying the leadership vision of *Everyone Can Lead*.

Fukinsei

asymmetry and imperfection.

Nature is neither symmetrical nor perfect. In the same way, there is no such thing as a perfect and all-inclusive form of leadership. Leadership is human and personal. As a result, it is unique but also has flaws. Fukinsei means letting go of inflexibility and embracing instead the beauty of perfect imperfection, so that others can participate in the creative process and thereby evolve towards something that is truly innovative and inspirational. In *Everyone Can Lead* we will examine both our strong and our less strong qualities, so that we can bring the very best that we have to offer to the surface. That will be our innovative and unique style of leadership.

簡素

Kanso *simplicity.*

Kanso means expressing things in a clear, simple and natural way. It reminds us not to think in terms of embellishment, but in terms of clarity, the kind of clarity that can only be achieved by omitting or excluding everything that is not essential. Simple is better; less is more! In this way, *Everyone Can Lead* reduces leadership to its essence: two simple basic principles that are pragmatic and easily applicable in practice, clearly illustrated with relevant examples and exercises.

考古

Koko *soberness.*

Koko places an emphasis on sobriety and austerity. Everything that is not necessary must be discarded. The aim is to create something that gives a feeling of focus and clarity. Koko also means that the personality and character of the artist are visible in his work. *Everyone Can Lead* shuns complex and externally imposed models and theories. My vision of leadership offers everyone the opportunity to develop their own personal form of leadership; the form that best expresses who they are.

Shizen *naturalness.*

Shizen means an absence of all pretension or artificiality, focusing instead on complete, unforced and creative intention. The aim is to find a balance between being part of nature, whilst at the same time distinguishing ourselves from it. Shizen seeks to foster natural behaviour that is neither contrived nor self-important, but is perfectly attuned to the impact and the results you wish to achieve. As a result, Authentic Adaptability plays an important role in *Everyone Can Lead*. You take your own nature as your starting point, but adjust it where necessary, consciously and sincerely, to reflect the context in which you find yourself.

Yugen *subtlety.*

Yugen means revealing more while showing less. In simple terms, the Zen vision involves making use of the power of suggestion; you always leave something to the imagination of the viewer. As you read this book, you will need to call on your own powers of imagination to create and shape your own form of leadership. The book will offer you principles and insights, but how you apply them is up to you. It is for you to decide how, where and when you want to lead.

Datsuzoku *freedom.*

Datsuzoku encourages you to escape from ordinariness and daily routine, allowing you to feel as though you have transcended the conventional and the banal. Once achieved, this results in a sensation of pleasant surprise and unexpected amazement. Whenever you break through a jaded pattern of behaviour, new creativity and inventiveness automatically come to the surface. If you make active use of this book, you will learn to recognise the old, often unconscious, habits that are holding you back, allowing you to replace them with new and more appropriate behaviour. Leadership means freely and deliberately choosing the action that seems most suitable in any given situation.

Seijaku *tranquillity.*

Seijaku brings a feeling of 'active rest' and calm into the hustle and bustle of daily life. Being in a state of active rest, with the calm and solitude this involves, makes it possible for you to find the essence of creative energy. In the hectic organisations that characterise the modern business world, this is perhaps the most difficult of the seven principles of wabi-sabi to apply. In *Everyone Can Lead*, calm and active rest are crucial elements for accurately assessing the context and your environment, thereby allowing you to implement the most appropriate leadership intervention. Last but not least, with this book I wish to help you to reflect in silence and repose on yourself, so that you can discover the very best versions of who you truly are. You cannot do this without seijaku.

FOREWORD

You don't need a title to be *a leader.* anonymous

Everyone leads. Your words and actions inevitably have an influence on the feelings and thoughts of others, which in turn has an influence on their words and actions. Sometimes this influence is conscious, more often it is unconscious. That brings us to the essence of this book: pausing to reflect on the ways in which your words and behaviour influence others and how you – can – lead them. Everything starts with self-awareness and self-insight. As the level of your self-insight continues to grow, you can use your influence and your leadership consciously to bring out the best in others. You do this by first starting with yourself, by being the best person you can possibly be. For me, that is what personal leadership means: bringing out the best in yourself and in others.

Via this book, I want to make clear how personal leadership can contribute towards meaning, happiness and well-being in the shape of personal satisfaction and excellent results. I believe that every person in an organisation can make a positive contribution, for himself, for his colleagues, and for the organisation as a whole. I have called this vision of leadership *The Leadership Connection.* Why? In part because Positive Connection is one of the basic principles in that vision and in part because I hope to create a connection between everyone who is favourable towards my vision. The Leadership Connection is a call to deal consciously with the influence that you possess. A call to bring out the best in yourself and in others. I sincerely hope that this book can 'lead' you towards your own form of personal leadership.

'Surely not another book about leadership?' I can hear some of you thinking. 'There are already so many!' Indeed there are, so many that it is almost impossible to keep count of their number. However, the vast majority of these books are about hierarchical leadership. You should already have understood from the preceding pages that The Leadership Connection is also about – in fact, primarily about – personal leadership. In this book, I will address everyone in an organisation, and not just its hierarchical leaders. In other words, personal leadership as the basis for all other forms of leadership. The Leadership Connection goes beyond the precepts of the standard models; it is a vision on leadership, a philosophy. With The Leadership Connection, I want to get back to the essence of leadership. To do this, I went in search of the two universal basic principles that form the foundations of good leadership: Positive Connection and Authentic Adaptability. I will offer you the necessary components to build up strong Positive Connections during your work. Authentic Adaptability means that you need to adjust your leadership style in your own way to meet the needs of the context and situation. This involves using different styles of leadership that you possess to respond in the best possible way to the prevailing circumstances, so that you can achieve the best possible results.

In the first instance, this book is experience based rather than evidence based. The book's vision is based on my own experience and the experiences of all the people I have worked with during the past thirty years. I have learnt much from positive examples and even more from less positive examples. *Everyone Can Lead* is therefore intended as a practical – and practice-based – book. At the same time, many of the elements in my vision are also supported by scientific research. What you will not find in this book, however, is perfection. Perfection does not exist. Or as the ensō symbol on the cover suggests: striving for perfection is already perfection. I am the first to admit that I regularly make mistakes in the application of my own vision. Each day I try to learn from these mistakes and to take another new step in the right direction. The Leadership Connection is a journey, not a destination.

The development and dissemination of The Leadership Connection is my way of giving meaning and purpose to what I do. I truly hope that The Leadership Connection can make a positive difference to you and your organisation. I will be a happy man if, by applying the basic principles and practices described in this book, you can focus more on the win-win combination of work satisfaction and excellent organisational results. By looking at leadership in the way I describe it in The Leadership Connection, I hope that I can help to set in motion a movement that 'leads' organisations and the people who work for them towards greater meaning, happiness and well-being. If we can achieve this, it will make not only the business world, but also the world in general a better place. I wish you enjoyable reading and a fascinating journey along the path that will guide you towards your own unique form of personal leadership.

Frans

▶ In this book I use numerous examples. They are all based on my own practical experience, but I have made them anonymous. In fact, many of the examples are based on a combination of situations. In this sense, they are realistic, but not real. Any similarity with existing people and/or organisations is purely coincidental.

In this book I use 'he', 'his' and 'him' when referring to persons. This makes the book more readable. I wish, however, to emphasise that I am addressing my words to everyone: male, female and gender neutral.

Finally, I would advise everyone to start reading this book from the beginning. It will provide you with useful information about, amongst other things, the 'why' of this book and also the role of leadership in the organisational context of today. If, however, you prefer to get straight down to putting my vision into practice, I suggest you start by going immediately to the section entitled 'Guiding principle 1 — Positive Connection'.

WHY A PRACTICAL HANDBOOK?

Leadership is
unlocking people's potential
to become *better.* Bill Bradley, former U.S. senator

The Leadership Connection brings leadership back to its essence: how can you bring out the best in yourself and others? This practical handbook will show how your personal leadership can lead to greater happiness and better results at work. Not only for you, but also for those around you.

For me, all forms of leadership start with personal leadership. For this kind of leadership, you don't need a team or a hierarchical 'boss'. Leadership is a process of positive influencing. As Luk Dewulf so perfectly expressed it in his book *Go with your talent*, personal leadership begins with doing what you like doing and what you are good at doing. In other words, bringing out the best in yourself. If you can combine this with making a Positive Connection with others, you will achieve a form of personal leadership that not only brings the best out of yourself, but also out of those others. Think, for example, of the difference between a receptionist who fails to say anything when people enter the office and a receptionist who wishes everyone a cheerful 'good morning' or 'good afternoon'. In the latter instance, the receptionist brings out the best in himself and in so doing creates a positive impact that brings out the best in others. That too is leadership – and it comes very close to what Mahatma Gandhi meant when he said: 'Be the change you want to see in the world.'

Via this book, I want to show you how and why leadership – bringing the best out of yourself and others – can make the best possible contribution to your own work satisfaction, to that of your colleagues and to the objectives of your organisation. The book is intended for everyone who is active in an organisation, whether as an individual employee or as a hierarchical leader, whether temporarily or permanently engaged, whether as a salaried member of staff or as a volunteer. Anyone and everyone can use this book to immediately take their first steps towards personal leadership. In the first instance, this will improve your personal work satisfaction. But you will soon notice that it also has a positive influence on your colleagues and your immediate environment. This is the real power of personal leadership. If you are a hierarchical leader, it is even more important that you bring out the best out in your people. You can do this either by attempting to rely exclusively on your hierarchical rank and title or else you can do it by demonstrating leadership based on who you are as a person. The respect and recognition that result from this latter option are always more effective than hierarchical authority and its associated punishments and rewards.

There are many different forms of personal leadership and hierarchical leadership. Choosing the form of leadership that is most suitable for you is crucial if you wish to find work satisfaction in what you do and to have a positive impact on others. Unfortunately, this is often where things go wrong. Many employees in organisations opt, often unconsciously, for forms and methods of working that are not well matched to their talents, preferences and personal style. These choices are made based on values and beliefs that are imposed on us by society, our upbringing and our environment. Values and beliefs that do not necessarily contribute to our work satisfaction. How many technical experts agree to take on a management role, only to discover that the extra salary in no way compensates for the resulting loss of job satisfaction? How many employees believe that they have little or no impact on their organisation? How many managers think that they always need to know all the answers? Instances of this kind have negative consequences, not only for the work satisfaction of the people in question, but also for the work satisfaction of their colleagues and for the effectiveness of the wider organisation. This book wants to show you the paths that you can follow in your pursuit of the form of leadership that is most appropriate for you and will allow you to bring out the best in yourself and those around you.

The basic question is therefore this: 'What kind of leader do you want to be?' This applies equally to both personal leadership and hierarchical leadership. What kind of impact do you want to have on your organisation? What contribution do you wish to make? These are all questions about meaning and happiness. Through your work in the organisation, how do you intend to find satisfaction in what you do and bring purpose to your life? There are many different forms of personal and hierarchical leadership that can help you to achieve this. Each of us has our own unique talents, preferences and style. In this book we will search together to find the best way for you to do your job and to discover how you can best be a leader in a manner that matches who you are.

My aim with this practical handbook is to help you to become the 'leader you want to be', the leader who can bring out the best in himself and in others. How will I do this? By sharing the insights that I have acquired during my long professional career. By passing on to you the basic principles and good practices that I have experienced over many years, not only first hand but also (and primarily) through the many people with whom I have had the privilege to work. By allowing you to discover possibilities and opportunities for improvement and by helping you to avoid potential pitfalls and traps. Moreover, by making this book a practical book, I have tried to ensure that the content will be as recognisable as possible. I have made no use of abstract, theoretical concepts, preferring to focus on simple basic principles that you can use in everyday practice. Even so, you need to remember that 'simple' is not the same as 'easy'. The simplest principles are often the most difficult to apply consistently in practice. For example, building on the (professional) ambitions, talents and preferences of your colleagues is much easier said than done. It requires attention, interest and time: resources that are increasingly scarce in our high-speed, high-intensity world.

Last but not least, for me this book is a way to return to the simplicity that embodies the essence of leadership. In recent years, I have seen far too many (and far too expensive) complex theories and leadership models that are supposed to have all the answers. I have seen too many organisations struggle painfully to push their people into the strait jacket of a uniform leadership model. I have seen too much human potential that remains wasted and unused. I have seen too many people lose their individuality by trying to conform to stereotypical views of leadership. Perhaps worst of all, I have seen far too many people who are unhappy in their work. For me, finding the best possible version of yourself and helping others to do the same is the fundamental basis of all leadership. As Leonardo da Vinci once said: 'Simplicity is the ultimate refinement.'

WHO IS THIS PRACTICAL HANDBOOK FOR?

For you

In the first instance, this book is addressed to every employee in every organisation. To everyone who is interested in finding greater meaning and greater happiness at work. Research demonstrates that 'bringing out the best in yourself' and 'making a difference' are two important factors for all of us, in terms of contributing to our motivation in the workplace. 'Autonomy' and 'connectedness' are two other motivational needs we all share. In the following pages, we will look in detail at these four key factors and how they can be exploited to everyone's benefit.

With the question 'What kind of leader do you want to be?', we will explore how you can bring out the best in yourself and in others. This means discovering the best form of personal leadership that matches who you are. The best possible version of yourself is the version that most closely reflects your talents, values and preferences and allows you to put them to maximum use. This is the first key factor for being motivated at work: doing the things you are good at and bringing out the best in yourself. If you do the things you are good at and you do them well, you will automatically inspire and motivate others to do the same, thereby becoming an important source of meaning for them. In this way, you can help to make a difference in your working environment, which is the second key motivational factor. For example, a forklift truck driver who drives his vehicle in an 'exemplary' manner can inspire his colleagues to do likewise. This not only benefits the drivers in question, but also the organisation for which they work. It further means that the contribution of the inspirational driver towards the organisation's success is not solely confined to the transportation of goods: he succeeds in improving the performance of the entire team.

This brings us automatically to the third factor that influences motivation at work: connectedness. The likelihood that others will follow the example of the 'good' truck driver is dependent on the extent to which he is trusted and respected. In this book, I will refer to this kind of connectedness as Positive Connection. The greater your level of Positive Connection, the greater the difference that you can make for others. Positive Connection gives you a double benefit: it makes you feel 'at home' in your place of work, whilst at the same time allowing you to contribute to greater meaning at work through the difference you are able to make for your colleagues and your organisation.

If the first three motivational success factors are in place, the fourth will ultimately follow. The better you are at your work and the more positive the influence that you are able to exert on others, the greater the likelihood that you will be given autonomy. If your organisation trusts you to do your job well without supervision and knows that you have an inspirational effect on the performance of others, your managers will be more inclined to give you more freedom to carry out your tasks in the manner that best suits your personal talents and preferences.

In this way, I hope that my practical handbook will help you to make a huge leap forward in terms of your motivation and your experience of meaning and satisfaction at work. A leap that will not only benefit you, but also your organisation.

That being said, I can well imagine that there are some readers who are not interested in the question: 'What kind of leader do you want to be?' Perhaps you have no ambitions to lead? Or perhaps you associate leadership with power, ego, status, office politics and other less attractive aspects of the hierarchical system of management? This is a reaction I can understand, because it cannot be denied that these less pleasant aspects do exist and are common to many organisations. However, in this book I am talking about personal leadership and therefore about personal influence and impact. And whether we like it or not, this is something that we all have, irrespective of whether we are aware of it or not. If you are in a bad mood tomorrow, so that you don't say a word during the weekly team meeting and just sit there with a face like thunder, you will inevitably have an effect on the other people at the table and on the way the meeting develops. Likewise, but in a more positive way, if you comment favourably on the proposal of a colleague during a presentation, you will have an effect not only on that colleague but also on everyone else in the room. Many of these influencing processes are unconscious. For this reason, in the following chapters it is my intention to prompt you to reflect consciously on the influence that you can have and would like to have on others. This, too, is a part of personal leadership and bringing out the best in both yourself and those around you.

In summary, the purpose of this book is to help you to successfully complete your search to discover the best possible version of yourself. It is a search that will not only contribute to your greater satisfaction at work, but also to greater satisfaction for your colleagues and better results for your organisation. Just as importantly, personal leadership will not only have an important impact on your working life, but also on your private life. The book will not explore this side of your life in any great detail, but many of the principles and practices that we will discuss can also be used in this private sphere. This can help you to view your relationships with your partner, your children, your parents, your family and your friends in a different light, opening the door for possible improvements. The choice is yours.

For you as a hierarchical leader

If you are a hierarchical leader, you have consciously chosen (or at least I hope you have consciously chosen) to lead others. As a result, you have a formal hierarchical relationship that gives you a degree of power over others. I realise that the word 'power' often has negative connotations, such as obligating, compelling, forcing, etc., and power can indeed be used in this way. We have probably all had experience of hierarchical leaders who 'rule' (rather than 'lead') on the basis of directive, obligatory and unilateral power that seeks to strike fear into the people who report to them.

For me, power means something different. I see power as 'the possibility to do something'. In other words, having the ability and the possibility to implement and complete certain tasks. Viewed in these terms, we all need power. If we wish to accomplish anything, we must have the power to initiate action, take decisions, involve others, etc. Power provides us with opportunities, but it also brings with it responsibilities. You need to constantly reflect on the manner in which you deal with your power. Perhaps the best example of this is to be found in the private sphere, where parents have a good deal of power over their children, especially while they are still young. The greater dependence of these young children means that they do not yet have the power to do things or take decisions for themselves. As a parent, you need to think carefully about how you use your power to assist your children in doing these things and making these decisions, preferably in the most constructive way possible. Exactly the same principle applies (or should apply) in hierarchical organisations.

If you interpret power as 'the possibility to do something', as a hierarchical leader you are in a privileged position not only to bring out the best in yourself, but also (and primarily) to bring out the best in others. This is one of the most important responsibilities that is frequently underestimated and, in my opinion, given too little attention. That importance and that need for attention is something that will be underlined repeatedly in this book. By focusing on the two guiding principles previously mentioned and on a number of practical 'tips and tricks', I will offer hierarchical leaders the necessary tools and methods to bring out the best in themselves as a leader and to bring out the best in the people that report to them. As such a leader, you can therefore be an important lever for improving both the work satisfaction of your staff and the overall business results of your organisation. It all depends on how you answer that key question: 'What kind of leader do you want to be?'

In the following chapters, you will learn how you can bring out the best in others on a basis of trust, respect, recognition, autonomy and purpose. This is what I refer to as Positive Connection. In other words, the members of your team will bring out the best in themselves and therefore contribute towards the team's objectives because they feel recognised and respected. Because they are trusted and given the autonomy that this trust entails. Because they believe in the mission and the objectives of the organisation and believe that their team can make a difference in this respect. We will examine in detail how you can build up this kind of Positive Connection. It is for you to decide how, when and where you want to start.

The higher the hierarchical position you occupy, the more severely others will assess and judge your Positive Connection with others. A general who has progressed through the ranks, who has shown that he understands and respects the world of his subordinates, who is modest about his abilities and achievements and who is an example of what he expects from others will receive much more respect and dedication from his people than a general who has been promoted for political reasons and who relies exclusively on his 'stars and stripes' to get things done. This is an analogy that can be applied to every organisation.

In addition to our key question — 'What kind of leader do you want to be?' — it is also possible for hierarchical leaders to ask themselves a second question: 'How do I want to be remembered by my people?' The answer to this question is different for everyone. Some people want to be remembered as being 'firm but fair'; others want to be remembered as 'empathic and supportive'; yet others as 'visionary and innovative'. The book does not impose any answers on this point. On the contrary, it is for each leader to use the components in the book to provide his own answer, based on how he wishes to use his own talents, values and preferences to give shape and form to his leadership. What things work well for you and what things are you less comfortable with? What makes you feel good and what makes you feel uneasy? What ambitions do you have for your 'legacy'? I will attempt to make you aware of your current approach, your desired approach, and the key differences between the two. What does the best version of yourself as a hierarchical leader actually look like? And what are the steps that will allow you to make that version a reality? All will be revealed in due course.

For you as a human resource manager

Reading this book as a human resource manager, you have a choice: you can apply its lessons either as an individual employee and/or as a hierarchical manager. In fact, a combination of both is not a bad idea: as a human resource manager it always pays to put yourself in the shoes of the employees, so that you can experience how the vision you plan to implement comes across.

In this introductory chapter I want to highlight in particular how you can use the book and the basic principles and practical methods it contains to introduce and develop a new leadership culture in your organisation. I had some doubts about whether I should write just a single section for human resource managers and CEOs combined. If you want to introduce a new culture, this inevitably means close collaboration between the CEO and/or the senior management team and the human resource department. In the end, I decided to write a separate section for each of them, because I believe that the CEO and the human resource manager both have a unique but ultimately different contribution to make to the process.

To start with, I would like to challenge the term 'human resources manager' or 'personnel manager'. These titles are not compatible with the vision of leadership that I bring in this book. If anyone is responsible for managing the employees, this is first and foremost the responsibility of the employees themselves. I regard this self-reliance as a crucial component of personal leadership. If there is anyone else who can be said to be responsible for the employee, this must in the first instance be the hierarchical leader. This aspect of hierarchical leadership is neatly encapsulated in the term 'people manager'. For this reason, I also much prefer the title 'HR business partner' to 'human resources manager'. This implies being a partner to both the individual employee and the hierarchical leader for the purpose of supporting them in their pursuit of the organisation's business objectives. Not so long ago, I was able to introduce a fine example of this vision into a major international organisation. In this organisation, the staff are now responsible for evaluating their own performance and for setting their future performance and development targets. The individual employees make all the necessary preparations for the review procedure and initiate the meeting with their line manager. The human resources department helps to make this process possible, in part by providing the necessary support and training that allows people to grow in their personal leadership. The hierarchical leaders are also given the necessary training and guidance in this same vision.

Although many HR business partners have learnt from Dave Ulrich that they should ideally play an important role as an 'employee champion', this is not an opinion I share. Rather than functioning as a champion for the employees, I am convinced that the role of the HR business partner is to stimulate the personal leadership of each individual employee, so that he can bring out the best in himself and in others. If the individual employee requires support and guidance to make this possible, this can potentially come from the HR business partner. However, such support and guidance have a more powerful effect if it comes from the hierarchical leader, with the HR business partner providing the necessary support and guidance to the hierarchical leader that will allow him to take on that role. This creates a self-supporting system, in which the role of the HR business partner is focused on facilitating and coaching. By adopting such a role as an HR business partner, you have enormous leverage. In this way, you can exert a much greater influence and create a much greater impact than when you are always the first point of contact for all the employees. In many companies, this necessitates resetting the content and the focus of the HR business partner's function. Leadership development, of both personal and hierarchical leadership, must become the driving force behind your personnel policy.

Introducing a priority for personal leadership as the basis for all forms of leadership in a company is by no means an easy task. You remove the possibility for employees to hide completely behind (bad) hierarchical leadership. Instead, the individual employees are made personally responsible for their own work satisfaction and their contribution to the organisation's results. This is a responsibility that not everyone is happy to accept. In this sense, perhaps you should see the introduction of this kind of system as a selection criterion for deciding which employees are a good fit for your organisation. However, it also needs to be emphasised that this new focus on the individual employees does not mean that the hierarchical leaders no longer have a role to play in the new leadership vision. They still have an exemplary personal leadership role of their own and they must continue to bring out the best in themselves and in others. Moreover, this is a role on which, in my opinion, hierarchical leaders should be assessed and judged. In a number of the companies with which I collaborate, the leaders are not only evaluated on the basis of their own performance, but also on the basis of their ability to successfully lead and develop others who work for them. The higher the position in the organisation, the greater the importance attached to this latter aspect.

Of course, you cannot achieve this overnight. People who have been used to working in a purely hierarchical system for years should not be thrown in at the deep end without the necessary degree of preparation and guidance. Introducing personal leadership takes time. It requires focus, awareness and support. It is not a quick win that will allow an organisation to reduce the number (and the cost) of its hierarchical leaders. I once worked with an organisation where the number of hierarchical managers was cut from eighty to twenty almost immediately, because it was assumed that all the teams and employees were now self-steering. Not surprisingly, the result was chaos and frustration. In my view, the supervision of the transition to personal leadership and the leadership vision as described in this book is a task best carried out by the HR business partner, in collaboration with the hierarchical leaders and the senior management team. But it needs to be repeated: this is not always an easy process. Many hierarchical leaders find it difficult to 'let go' of their employees and are reluctant to encourage personal leadership, often seeing this (initially, at least) as a loss of control. Consequently, a transition of this kind will only succeed if it is accompanied by a combination of the necessary boldness with patience, understanding and support. At the end of the day, all the effort will be worth it, because there are benefits for all concerned, including the organisation as a whole.

With this book, I want to provide the HR business partner or HR expert with the means to make the transition to the leadership vision described in this book as easy as possible. The book clearly describes the basic principles and the most important practices for both individual employees and hierarchical leaders. Using these elements, it is a relatively simple task to redefine the different roles and responsibilities in all relevant HR processes. For example, you can add the question 'What kind of leader do you want to be?' to all your recruitment and promotion processes. This takes things a stage further and goes much deeper than behaviour-oriented interviews and (psycho)technical tests. In my vision of leadership, 'wanting to' is just as important as 'being able to'. In a similar vein, you can give the employees a leading role in performance and career management processes, by allowing them to assess their own leadership and that of their colleagues. Or you can use your employee satisfaction surveys to check the levels of trust, respect, recognition, autonomy and purpose in your organisation. The possibilities are almost endless. By using this book, you can help your people to gain insight into their talents, values and preferences in relation to personal and hierarchical leadership. This will allow them to design their own development trajectory, a trajectory that will lead them to the best possible version of themselves. This, too, is an element of personal leadership.

Looking at leadership in the manner that I describe it in this book means looking at every single employee in your organisation in a different way and from a different perspective. It means seeing and appreciating the richness of diversity amongst these employees and focusing on the unique contribution that each of them can make. It means abandoning the strict and uniform leadership models that are still so often employed today. It means adopting a new form of leadership in which every individual, whether he occupies a hierarchical position or not, brings out the best in himself and stimulates others to do the same. This is the way that leads to greater workplace happiness and better results.

For you as a CEO

As a CEO, you may — and probably should — read and apply the lessons of this book as a hierarchical leader. You should never underestimate the extent to which you are seen as an example in your organisation, and especially in the field of personal and hierarchical leadership. As the legendary basketball player and coach John Wooden once said: 'There is no more powerful leadership tool than your own personal example.' I experienced precisely this kind of effect at first hand at the end of the 1990s, when all the male staff at the company where I was then working received a mail from the personnel department to inform us that we no longer needed to wear a tie at work. It was only required when dealing with outside visitors or on other more formal occasions. Even so, on the day after the mail was circulated all the men still arrived at the office wearing a tie. They all looked up the chain of hierarchical command to see what their (male) line managers intended to do. This process ended at the top of the hierarchical ladder with the CEO, and because his function of dealing with external visitors every day required him to always wear a tie, everyone else in the organisation decided to follow suit. Until the following summer. It was then so warm that even the CEO finally took off his tie and rolled up his shirt sleeves. Within the hour, all the company's male employees had done the same! From that day on, casual dress in the company was a fact.

As the CEO, you report to the board of directors or to the people or entities who own the organisation. They expect you to use the resources allocated to you, including the organisation's employees, in the most effective and efficient manner. This book can help you to fulfil that expectation. How? In my vision, I regard every employee as a leader and define leadership as the ability to bring out the best in yourself and in others. If, as the CEO, you support and facilitate this process, you will automatically maximise the use of the human potential that your organisation possesses — which is not what currently happens in most organisations. Research has shown that worldwide as many as 85% of all employees feel only moderately engaged or not engaged at all towards their organisation, as a result of which they do not make full use of their potential. By bringing out the best in your people, you help to develop employees who make the best possible use of their talents and who focus on doing the things they like to do and therefore do well. This in turn maximises the likelihood that these employees will influence others to likewise bring out the best in themselves. In other words, this kind of leadership is self-reinforcing: leaders create leaders.

One complaint that I regularly hear from CEOs and boards of directors is that employees at all levels of the organisation display too little initiative. They expect their people to show more 'entrepreneurship', a word that you will find in the value charters of many organisations nowadays. In fact, there is also a new term that specifically describes the display of entrepreneurship within a large organisation: intrapreneurship. On the other side of the debate, if you ask employees in organisations why their behaviour tends to be reactive instead of proactive, the answer you will often get is: 'My boss prefers to do/decide that himself'. Or: 'I am not given enough autonomy to act independently'. Or: 'They don't trust me to do it on my own'. Or: 'My boss always wants to do it his own way'. And so on. In my experience, employees are frequently capable of displaying lots of entrepreneurship, but as their leader you have to have the guts to let them go. Giving them the necessary freedom to act takes courage and audacity. In this book, I will describe how this courage and audacity can be used to build Positive Connections with your employees. Leadership connections based on trust, respect, recognition, autonomy and purpose so that your employees can bring out the best in themselves. This means that you have to have confidence in your employees and must be open to the use of alternative ways to achieve the results you all desire. Research has often shown that diversity can lead to better results, but only if everyone respects and values the different approaches to which diversity leads.

By introducing personal leadership into your leadership culture and by regarding everyone as a leader in his own right, you send out a powerful message to the organisation for which you, as CEO, are ultimately responsible. It implies that you expect everyone to be a role model and to set an example, whilst at the same time underlining that everyone in the organisation can make a difference and is there-fore capable of making an important contribution to the organisation's results. It is almost as if you give everyone 'permission' to bring out the best in themselves and in others. For many organisations this means a massive cultural change. Changing a culture takes time and needs examples of the new norms, values and behaviour that others can then follow. Culture is embodied in the stories that people tell. One of the companies I work with has been investing in continuous improvement for more than forty years. This process is embedded deep in their culture and was created by the company's founder, who encouraged (and still encourages) his peo-ple to be 'positively dissatisfied'. This is his way of ensuring that his team contin-ually question everything they do in a positive and constructive manner, so that further improvements can be made.

As a CEO, you will need courage and perseverance if you wish to introduce the leadership culture described in this book into your organisation. But I have no hes-itation in guaranteeing you that your board of directors, shareholders, customers and competitors will notice the difference, not only in terms of your business re-sults but also in terms of positive personal contact with your employees.

As we look ahead into the next century, leaders will be those who empower others. Bill Gates

HOW DID THIS PRACTICAL HANDBOOK COME ABOUT?

In theory there is no difference between theory and practice. In *practice* there is. Yogi Berra

This book is a handbook. A practical guide. In the following pages you will not find any expensive, revolutionary or complex theories. It is based on my own experience and insights and, above all, the experiences and insights of all the people I have met during my career: colleagues, leaders, customers, participants in my courses and coachees. My roles over the years as an IT project manager, talent director, coach, trainer and consultant put me in a privileged position to experience at first hand the challenges of work, career development, personal development, personal leadership and hierarchical leadership. During that time, I also had the privilege of supporting many organisations in their roll-out of my vision on leadership.

My own leadership story, like the stories of many of the people I have worked with, was far from being sunshine and roses all the way. Fortunately, most of these stories (mine included) eventually contained their fair share of roses, but often mixed with a liberal sprinkling of thorns. In my case, for example, I was brought up to believe that 'making it in life' was the key to happiness. This 'making it' meant a senior position with a good salary in a respected organisation. I pursued this goal for years and all it got me was burn-out at the age of thirty-three. It was a hard and painful lesson that not only had a serious impact on me, but also on the most precious people around me, especially my partner. This was the turning point in my professional life and the start of my intention to put work satisfaction before money and status. Even so, it took me many years and several more ups and downs before I could finally leave my old habits and convictions behind me for good. What's more, my initial pursuit of 'success' was not the only mistake I made in my career. I soon learnt that living and working in keeping with your own personal talents, values and preferences is a life-long challenge that never goes away.

This book bundles together the most important lessons and insights I have been able to collect over the years. These experiences and stories have frequently taught me how not to do things. Sadly, that is sometimes one of the more thankless aspects of leadership: good personal and hierarchical leadership often seems to be self-evident. If you work together with colleagues or leaders who succeed in giving the best of themselves and in bringing out the best in others, everything seems to work perfectly, almost of its own accord. When this happens, the role of the leader is not central. In fact, it sometimes seems that he has done nothing special to contribute to his team's success. His people experience a fine and productive working environment that almost seems to have materialised out of nothing. Automatically. As a matter of course. However, it is a very different story when good leadership principles and practices are ignored. It is only then that people realise just how damaging poor leadership can be and just how important good personal and hierarchical leadership truly are. In this way, I have not only learnt from my own mistakes, but also from the mistakes that I have seen others make.

I have been able to apply and test the principles and practices contained in this book in many of the different companies I have worked with in recent years. Not just with CEOs, directors and senior managers. Not just with experts in leadership. But also (and primarily) with individual employees at all different organisational levels. All these influences contributed towards my wish to write a practical handbook to personal and hierarchical leadership that is 'down-to-earth'. A pragmatic and no-nonsense guide, modelled on reality as experienced in organisations today.

In other words, this book is not the result of decades of scientific research and complex statistical analyses. These elements certainly have their place in the study of leadership and the making of recommendations to improve it. However, my background as a mathematician and an IT specialist obliges me to say that the complexities, variables and factors that affect leadership are so numerous that they can never be integrated into a single model. Of course, many of the arguments in this book are supported by scientific theory and evidence, but my starting point has always been the daily practice. The scientific substantiation (which I was usually able to find, anyway) was only a secondary consideration. You can find more details about this scientific background by consulting the reading list at the end of the book.

A practical handbook of this kind can never be definitive. Each new day I am confronted by new situations and new stories, which allow me to acquire new insights. This is true for everyone. The search for the best possible version of yourself is a journey, not a final destination. As a result, I hope that this practical handbook will accompany you not only on the current stage of your journey, but will help to further your personal development throughout the rest of your professional career. You can see it as a rich collection of insights from which you can choose as seems most appropriate and to which, over the years, you can add new insights of your own.

HOW CAN YOU USE THIS PRACTICAL HANDBOOK?

A book is a *gift* you can open again and again. Garrison Keillor

Nobody ever learnt to play the piano or ride a bicycle by reading a book. The same is true of this book. It will offer you insights, basic principles and good practices, but this does not mean that you will be able to apply them immediately. I like the proverb 'Practice makes progress'. You need to translate these insights, principles and practices into your own reality in your own organisation. This will take time, but the important thing is to get started straight away. You need to practice and experiment. You need to have the courage to question yourself and to make changes, or even to start all over again, if necessary. And while this kind of practice is indeed crucial, you should forget the old proverb 'Practice makes perfect'. No one and nothing is perfect. This was one of my own personal pitfalls. For many years, I struggled to find perfection in everything I did. I now know that perfection does not exist. There is no such thing as a perfect job and there is no such thing as a perfect leader. Searching to find the best possible version of yourself is a never-ending story, and one that will inevitably be filled with ups and downs. As I have already mentioned, I am the first to admit that I still regularly make mistakes when applying my own leadership vision. Personal development means working to improve yourself, day after day. That is why I wanted to make my book a practical handbook. It provides you with exercises to discover and develop your own insights, your own basic principles and your own practices. It will allow you to experiment with the things that work for you and will show you the things that do not work. In short, it will help you on your way to find the best possible version of yourself.

You can approach the book in different ways. In my experience, most people prefer to read a book of this kind from start to finish, before attempting to apply the various themes and exercises that seem most relevant to them. During this first read-through, these readers mark the sections to which they want to return later on. Completing the exercises they have selected demands a good deal of introspection. You have to look deeply at your own behaviour and dare to question its appropriateness. This is by no means easy. We all have our 'blind spots', in the sense of strengths or points for development of which we are not aware. For example, you might think that you are an assertive communicator, whereas others think you are aggressive. Or you regard yourself as only a moderate organiser, while others think you are an organisational genius.

The only way to gain information about these blind spots is to ask for feedback from others. In an organisational context, this means asking for such feedback from your colleagues, your manager, your team members, your internal and external clients, etc.: in short, everyone who has a good idea about who you are and how you behave within the organisation. In practice, it should not be difficult to get this kind of feedback. All it takes is a short e-mail or conversation asking for people to comment on your strong and less strong points. If you prefer, you can ask them to limit their comments to a specific theme or a specific aspect of your behaviour. You will find that most people are happy to oblige. The feedback they give you is a mine of useful information. See it as a valuable present, even when (or perhaps especially when) it points to matters where you still need to develop. Feedback is, of course, always a matter of someone's personal perception. But if several people give you the same feedback, you can be fairly sure that in this instance their perception equates to reality. So what does all this mean? It means that when you start using this practical handbook, it is a good idea to collect feedback from various people on the themes that you marked during your initial read-through. And always remember to thank your respondents for their feedback, even when you do not agree with it.

Making use of what you have learnt and applying your new intentions in practice is probably the most important step to getting the most out of this handbook. But it is often the most difficult step. My advice is not to be too ambitious. It is often better to first focus on one or two themes rather than trying to do too much all at once. 'Petit pas à petit pas', (step-by-step) as the French say, is often the most effective approach.

Many of the things we do are habits. The way we greet others, they way we present ourselves, the way we behave in meetings, the way we work with others, etc. Over the years, these things have become second nature to us, as comfortable as an old shoe. Habits are not easy to change. It is almost as if they have been programmed into our brains. If you want to work in a new way, this means that you need to delete the old programme and install a new one. This requires a conscious and deliberate effort, which can sometimes be difficult, if, for example, you are under pressure and/or need to act quickly. For this reason, it is often a good idea to try and find a 'buddy', a good colleague or friend who is aware of your new intentions and can encourage you when you are moving in the right direction or can warn you when you are slipping back into your former 'bad' habits. For instance, if it is your intention to listen more and interrupt less during meetings, the buddy can give you a metaphorical (and sometimes literal) 'kick under the table' the next time you butt in when someone is talking.

Of course, although this kind of buddy is useful, he is not essential. There is no reason why you cannot start using this book alone. That being said, I think we all know that making a journey together with someone else is preferable to making a journey on our own. And in this case, it will also provide more powerful and more lasting results. You can compare it, for example, with a time management workshop. If you are the only one to follow the workshop and then try afterwards to apply the new techniques that are now familiar to you but are still unfamiliar to everyone else in your team, the results are likely to be frustrating. You attempt to work undisturbed for a period by closing the door of your office, but your colleagues keep on barging in. You say you want no meetings scheduled for a Friday afternoon, so that you have time to plan for the following week, but your colleagues plan one anyway. You say that you intend to answer mails only twice per day but your colleagues still insist on an answer within five minutes... If you are not careful, the same thing can happen when you attempt to apply the principles and practices in this book. For this reason, it is better to work in tandem with others. If you all know each other's objectives and action plans, if you can suggest corrections to each other where necessary and if you can celebrate successes together, you will be able support each other on your common journey and the outcome will be more pleasant and much more productive.

This is the kind of handbook that will often disappear into the cupboard for a time, only to be pulled out again at regular intervals. It is not possible to apply everything in the book all at once. You should first focus on the aspects that are currently most important for you in your personal context and in your organisation. Tomorrow is another day and will perhaps confront you with new challenges, a new working environment or new needs and objectives. When that happens, open your cupboard, get out this handbook and see how it can help you to become the best possible version of yourself in the new context. This will bring you into contact with other insights, other principles and other practices.

I hope that this practical handbook will accompany you throughout your journey, wherever it might lead you. I hope that you will make notes in it, showing how and when and why you used it with success, but also scrapping the things that did not work in your particular case. Because it is certain that not everything will go exactly the way you planned. Going in search of your best possible self is a complex and highly personalised task, full of twists, turns and detours. So if you dislike books full of dog-eared pages and scribbled comments, you had better buy two copies: one to work in and one to read!

WHAT IS LEADERSHIP?

Leadership is not about titles, positions, or flow charts. It is about one life *influencing* another. John C. Maxwell

Before we discuss my Leadership Connection definition of leadership, it may be useful to first explore the more traditional definitions and assumptions.

If you look at the origins of the word 'lead' and its equivalents in various North European languages (*lædan* in Old English, *leidon* in Old Dutch, *laid-jan* in Proto-German), they all have basically the same original meaning: 'guide', 'at the front', 'showing the way', even 'setting an example'. It is worth noting that none of these terms implies a hierarchical relationship. The guide is not necessarily the boss. You could say that it is similar to how you use a modern GPS system. You indicate where you want to go, whether you want the fastest or the shortest route, what intermediary locations you wish to pass en route, etc. The GPS then 'leads' you like a guide to your chosen destination. Whilst always taking account of your preferences, the GPS itself chooses the roads you have to 'follow'. But you will only do this if you have confidence that the GPS will effectively bring you to the right destination in the manner you require.

Traditionally, the leader in an organisation is seen as the person who decides that organisation's destination and therefore sets its vision. A strategy is then devised that will allow the organisation to follow a path that will lead to the successful realisation of the vision. The leader also often controls the speed at which the organisation and its people move along that path. Once this happens, the leader is regarded as being hierarchically superior to the others. Most leaders are expected to provide the necessary framework that will allow continuous progress along the path to be made. Some leaders take this framing process to extremes. They plan every step along the way, including the necessary timings, roles and responsibilities, and then look constantly over everyone's shoulder to check that everything is happening as it should. It is hardly surprising, then, that this kind of approach has resulted in the development of terminology like 'human resources', which suggests (as it were) that people are machines that need to be directed. You might be forgiven for thinking that some leaders have more confidence in their GPS than in their own employees: at least the GPS gets to choose its own route.

If you are this kind of leader, who directs his people from point A to point B and then from point B to point C and so on, you are missing a huge opportunity, because in this way you will fail to use the full potential that your people possess. Let's consider the GPS comparison again. The GPS knows every road on the map and is therefore more than capable of deciding the best route. And so that is what you let it do. As the leader in an organisation, however, it is very unlikely that you will know all the possible roads that can lead to your desired objective and equally unlikely that you can assess with 100% accuracy the potential of all your employees, and certainly not in the VUCA (volatile, uncertain, complex and ambiguous) world in which we now live. No doubt some of your employees know parts of the map better than you do. If you are prepared to allow these employees to help decide the route, you will be able to combine all those different parts of the map together, to create the best possible total map. At the same time, you can also check to see who is best at travelling along the different kinds of roads and in what kinds of vehicles. In this way, you not only find the best route for your journey as a whole, but also ensure that your people will be able to find their own way around any obstacles that they encounter en route. If I am driving on 'my' part of the map, there is a good chance that I already know all the alternative side roads that will allow me to bypass any obstacles and still get me safely to the right destination. But if the leader tries to decide the route all by himself, his map might lead me to obstacles of which I am not aware and where I am less able to find alternative solutions. When this happens, the leader's road to the organisation's destination may turn out to pain and frustration...

This is, of course, an oversimplification. It is not possible for everyone within an organisation to choose his own route to arrive at the organisation's objectives.

This requires a degree of alignment and coordination. At the same time, you cannot afford to spend the endless amount of time that is necessary to wait until a consensus supported by everyone has been reached. The modern world moves too fast for that. This is probably one of the most important challenges facing the leaders of today's organisations: finding the right balance between speed and engagement. There is an old African proverb which says: 'If you want to go fast, go alone. If you want to go far, go together'. By definition, organisations bring people together. So if you want to go a long way, you know what you need to do. Remember also that slower in the beginning often means faster at the end. This was something that I discovered during my period as an IT project manager. If you make a mistake at the start of a project through too much haste, it can cost you a lot in terms of time and money to correct things later on. Spending more time on analysis at the beginning usually means that the project is completed more quickly.

But let us return to the origin of the word 'leader', in the sense of being a guide. A guide is always free to determine with his fellow travellers both the nature of the destination and the best way to get there. Moreover, the guide does not always need to walk in front of everyone. Whoever knows a particular stretch of road better than anyone else is the one who should be doing the leading. This means that more than one person can show the others the way, making it possible to switch flexibly between the different travellers. In other words, at different times everyone can be both follower and leader.

Before finishing this section, I would like to offer one final metaphor: ballroom dancing. As with all dancing, the music determines the rhythm. The route to be followed around the dance floor and the way that the route is followed was traditionally determined by the man, who 'led'. In the past, this meant that women who wanted to lead had to dance with other women. Fortunately, times have changed and couples now decide between themselves who will lead. Depending on the music, the rhythm, the dancers' preferences and the mutual agreements they make, this results in almost constant variation, which simply serves to enhance the beauty and the pleasure of the dancing. Even in modern dance culture, where people nowadays are more inclined to dance individually, it is still possible for everyone to lead. The person with the most original or the most entertaining moves can often persuade others to follow in his footsteps (or dance steps), sweeping them into action on the wave of his enthusiasm. You can see a good example of this on YouTube™: youtube.com/watch?v=GA8z7f7a2Pk. Watch the full three minutes!

THE ORGANISATIONAL CONTEXT

Without context words and actions have no *meaning* at all. Gregory Bateson

Before looking at how my vision can be applied through The Leadership Connection, it will be useful to first examine the general context of leadership as it exists in organisations today. If we look at what takes place in this context, at the various influences and situations that currently predominate, we can see that three important evolutions form the basis for recent developments and trends: the impact of technology, doing more with less, and the scarcity of talent.

A VUCA world

The role of technology is one of the most important reasons why we nowadays talk so much about a VUCA world. This acronym stands for Volatile, Uncertain, Complex and Ambiguous.

Technology has increased the speed of everything, but in particular the speed of change, to a level that sometimes makes it difficult for us humans to follow. One of the consequences is that organisations often no longer have the time to let all the decisions be taken by people at the top of the hierarchical ladder. As a result, individual employees and teams are nowadays being given greater decision-making powers nowadays, because this is the only way for the organisation to act and react with sufficient speed. For example, production staff can now carry out minor repairs to their machines without the need to wait for the maintenance technicians. This evolution means that you can appeal increasingly to your employees' personal leadership by giving them more autonomy to make decisions.

Technology has already automated all the simple tasks, so that the non-automated tasks that remain are nearly all complex in nature. In fact, the complexity of products and services is now so great that no single person can be expected to know all the answers. Whereas in the past people looked to their hierarchical leaders to solve complex problems, today employees are expected to take the initiative to get all the people necessary to deal with the problem around the same table with a minimum of delay. Consider the way your bank works. Nowadays, you hardly ever get to see your bank manager (which was often the case in the past), but instead are seen by the specialist who can best respond to your request for a loan, investment advice, insurance, etc. In other words, your contact person at the bank will ensure that you get the help you need from the specialist that is best able to provide it. This, too, is personal leadership.

It is often said that technology has turned the world into a village, where even relatively small events can have a huge and wide-ranging impact. The current (2020-2021) COVID-19 pandemic is a good example of the VUCA world in which we are living. Even after almost two years, the way the virus works and is transmitted is still not fully known. We hear contradictory opinions from scientists about the best preventative measures, while governments introduce new guidelines with increasing frequency, none of which is 100% watertight. The result is universal uncertainty and ambiguity. Hospitals, care homes, schools and business organisations are all left to decide how best to interpret and implement the sometimes conflicting advice and instructions they are being given. This requires leadership based on solidarity, respect and trust. It means that everyone needs to pull in the same direction in order to stem the advance of the pandemic and that everyone needs to take personal responsibility for his own environment, even if this sometimes means having to remind colleagues of the responsibilities that they also need to take. This is a fine example of how personal leadership can really make a difference.

A VUCA world makes leadership more difficult but also more important. Every aspect of leadership, from the creation of a vision and the setting of a good example to the taking of decisions and the provision of support for your people, demands far more attention and involves far greater complexity than ever before. As a result, good leadership has never been more challenging – or more necessary.

More with less

If there is one mantra that I come across in almost every organisation that I work with, it is this: 'More with less'. More output, profits, etc. (preferably with no loss of quality or speed), but with less resources. If you combine this with the fact that labour costs are the largest item of expenditure in almost every organisation, you don't need to be a financial genius to see where CEOs and boards of directors first look to make cuts. As a result, automation and computerisation have already replaced a great deal of human labour. Until now, it has largely been simple (and often boring, repetitive) tasks that have been taken over by computers and machines, but in the future more complex tasks will also be tackled. What's more, it doesn't stop there. In addition to automation, organisations have also tried to find other ways to cut their personnel costs. The number of management levels has been drastically reduced, resulting in flatter and leaner organisational structures. Consequently, there are no longer any 'assistant manager' or 'assistant director' positions, which in the past allowed people to grow gradually into their hierarchical leadership role. Nowadays, the progression from team leader to head of department to managing director often involves just a few short steps. We expect our hierarchical leaders to hit the ground running. This makes it all the more important for every employee to think seriously in advance about our key question: 'What kind of leader do you want to be?' Do you really want that hierarchical leadership role and, if so, how will you approach it? Or do you prefer to remain as an individual employee, who makes a contribution by giving shape and form to his personal leadership in a different way?

In organisations that work with self-steering teams, this vision is taken much further. Almost all hierarchical leadership positions have been replaced by team coaches and personal leadership. Teams decide for themselves how they plan their activities: who does what, where and when, who accepts responsibility for the various tasks that need to be performed, etc. This is a fine concept, at least in theory, but it is often difficult to implement in practice, especially in organisations that have been structured hierarchically for decades. Personal leadership and conflict resolution skills are two absolute conditions for any organisation that hopes to make a success of self-steering teams. And the more organisations are flattened through the elimination of hierarchical levels, the greater the importance of personal leadership becomes.

The scarcity of talent

The current scarcity of talent on the labour market is another good reason for organisations to invest in leadership. Whereas in the past employers could usually select new recruits from a wide range of candidates, and therefore had the power in their hands, we now live in a world where this power has passed into the hands of the job seekers. The war for talent is over, and talent has won. It is generally known and accepted that bad hierarchical leadership is one of the most important reasons why people leave an organisation. This underlines just how crucial good leadership can be, if you want to recruit and retain the right (and fully engaged) employees.

The fact that employees now have a wide range of choice about where and for whom they work means that they are no longer afraid to go in search of the organisations that offer them the things they want. In response to this changed situation, organisations now focus on four elements that have been shown to be key factors in motivating all employees, both potential and existing: mastery, autonomy, purpose (or meaning) and connection.

Mastery means being able to make maximum use of your talents, bringing out the best in yourself and exploring/developing your potential to the full. Autonomy is closely linked to mastery: you are given (joint) control over your tasks and are able to implement them independently. At work, there is nothing quite so pleasing as doing things the way you want to do them. Purpose is the new happiness. The happiness myth has exploded, with most people now understanding that lasting happiness is not something we are likely to find in this world. Happiness only occurs momentarily at best, and when that happens you need to seize those moments and enjoy them. Having a purpose can continue to make your life worthwhile, even during those moments when you are not happy. Organisations have, by definition, the potential to provide purpose. They bring together a group of people to pursue and successfully achieve the same mission. It is not without good reason that Simon Sinek recommends that you should always start with the 'why' of organisations. Last but not least, connection with others is a basic human need. Being part of a like-minded group of people puts you at ease. You feel at home, recognised and accepted. You have your own place in a network of people that supports you and offers you safety. These are fundamental evolutionary impulses, which date back to the dawn of time, when such connection was vital for survival in a cruel and dangerous world.

As an organisation, you can (and should) focus on these four elements to create a motivating work environment for your employees. By now, I am sure that you have already understood that personal and hierarchical leadership can play an important role in making this possible.

THE LEADERSHIP CONNECTION

The most powerful **leadership** tool you have is your own *personal example*. John Wooden

My definition of leadership

In **The Leadership Connection** I define leadership as:

**'a process of self-insight and positive influencing
with the aim of bringing out the best in yourself and in others,
in order to achieve the objectives of the organisation.'**

Everyone can be a leader

Positive influencing means that your attitude, actions and words positively influence the attitude, actions and words of others. In other words, leadership is not exclusively a matter of hierarchical relationships. Each and every one of us constantly influences others in our environment, often unconsciously. Making use of your positive influence consciously by being the best possible version of yourself is what I call personal leadership. In this way, for example, a production operative who strictly follows the safety guidelines can inspire his colleagues to do the same. And the more respect and trust this worker enjoys amongst those colleagues, the greater the likelihood that this will happen. This brings us to the first guiding principle of The Leadership Connection: the power of Positive Connection, or bringing out the best in others by bringing out the best in yourself.

> The first guiding principle is Positive Connection . Positive Connections are based on trust, respect, recognition, autonomy and purpose. Not on power and fear. Positive Connections are something you can invest in and build up. The stronger the Positive Connection, the stronger the mutual positive influencing can be.

Much of this mutual influencing happens unconsciously. Think of how you sometimes clear the snow away from the pavement in front of your house, only to see your neighbour do the same thing a quarter of an hour later, inspired (consciously or unconsciously) by the example you have set. The purpose of The Leadership Connection is to make you aware of your influence, thereby allowing you to use it in a positive and constructive way, so that the process of mutual influencing can contribute to the greatest possible extent towards the mission of your organisation and the work satisfaction of you and your colleagues. This requires the necessary degree of self-insight, which brings us to the second guiding principle: Authentic Adaptability.

> The second guiding principle is Authentic Adaptability . Leadership must be authentic, whilst at the same time being adjusted to reflect the context, the situation, the people involved, the nature of the work, the timing, the organisational culture, etc. As a result, there is no single, uniform and all-inclusive model or style of leadership. Leadership is the continuous use of the best possible version of yourself, depending on the context, situation and desired impact.

Put briefly, in The Leadership Connection I see leadership as a balancing act between being true to your own personal preferences and adjusting your actions to the context and the relevant objectives. You can compare it to walking a tightrope, in which the rope is the Positive Connection between you and the other(s) involved. The stronger the connection, the more powerful the influence.

The purpose of bringing out the best in yourself and stimulating others to do the same is to achieve the results that the organisation desires. It is these results that give direction and purpose to Positive Connection and Authentic Adaptability. Moreover, this has the double benefit of not only realising the organisation's objectives, but also improving the sense of fulfilment, happiness and well-being of everyone who works for the organisation.

Please note that in none of these definitions do I make mention of titles, functions, personality characteristics, leadership styles and/or models. There are many different roads to good leadership and everyone can be a leader.

I first met Tim in a meeting with the human resource department of a large industrial organisation. Tim is one of the people who provide technical training for the organisation's staff. During the meeting, he introduced himself very briefly and thereafter kept his comments to an absolute minimum, in a manner that bordered on the surly. It was clear that he was waiting critically to see what this meeting with the 'flash consultant' would actually bring. His attitude made it equally clear that he would not be impressed by 'expensive consultant talk'. This is where Tim and I were able to find a connection. If there is one aspect of my work on which I constantly hammer it is the power of common sense. Like Tim, I am not interested in expensive words; I am interested in getting things done.

As part of the project we were working on, a number of the employees were obliged to change jobs within the organisation. The introduction of various automated processes meant that several people from the production section had to take on a new function in the warehouse, which had been expanded in recent years, and this transition involved the need for significant retraining. In other words, the employees in question were faced with the prospect of an intense and technically challenging training course. As you might expect, not all of them viewed this prospect with enthusiasm — and that's putting it mildly!

It was Tim's task to mentor these people during their transition to their new job. He had worked for more than 25 years in the production section and knew it like the back of his hand. But because the work in this section was becoming too physically demanding for him, a few years ago the human resource manager had asked Tim to think about switching to a position in the training team. This was not an easy decision for him to take and his main concern was whether or not he had the ability to do the training job properly. With the necessary support from the human resource manager, he finally decided to take the plunge. Since then, he had become more than competent at the organisation and implementation of technical training courses. For the current transition, he had also devised an excellent conversion trajectory for the people from the production section, working in collaboration with several experts from the warehouse facility.

But Tim's contribution went much further than the re-training programme. He knew the production section and the people who worked there through and through. For this reason, he decided to approach the people affected by the transition personally, so that he could reassure them and deal with any concerns they might have. In most organisations, this kind of transition frequently leads to heated objections and protracted negotiations with the unions, but in this case Tim's personal intervention helped to create a constructive dialogue and had a positive impact on the attitudes of those involved. The production employees trusted and respected Tim and in his own style he brought them an open and honest message, which they were able to appreciate. He did not pretend that the training would be easy, but told them that he would be there to support them every step of the way and that they could count on him.

This, indeed, is Tim's strength. He always commits himself 100% to help production workers who opt to make the switch to a job in the warehouse. He encourages them when the going gets tough, but also checks to ensure that they are making the necessary effort. In this way, he is fair to both his trainees and the organisation. As a result, the employees always feel that Tim has their best interests at heart, even when he has to communicate difficult news. With Tim, you often hear them say, you always know where you stand; there are no unexpected surprises. Moreover, once 'his' trainees have actually started work in the warehouse, Tim often pops in to see how they are getting on, demonstrating genuine interest in their welfare in their new environment.

By bringing out the best in himself, Tim knows how to bring out the best in others. Day after day, he practises his own style of leadership, not based on any hierarchical role, but on the supportive nature of his behaviour. This is personal leadership at its best. Tim works quietly and modestly, and never boasts about what he achieves, but the recognition he receives from his colleagues in both production and the warehouse speaks volumes about the importance of his role. Today, Tim is one of the most respected members of the training team and makes a crucial contribution to the credibility and good reputation of the organisation's human resource department.

It goes without saying that Tim had no need of my 'consultancy'. In fact, we took his approach as an example to be extended to several other reorganisation trajectories in the transition project as a whole. I learnt a lot about leadership from Tim. I still see him from time to time and we greet each other briefly, in our common style. Our no-nonsense connection made during that first meeting still persists and our respect for each other has continued to grow. This creates a bond that often requires no more than a short but meaningful nod and a look of mutual understanding.

Leaders create leaders

Leaders don't create followers, they create more leaders. Tom Peters

There has been much discussion in the literature and elsewhere about whether true leaders actually create followers or leaders. The Leadership Connection is in no doubt: leaders create new leaders. In this vision, the act of following results in people being inspired to bring out the best in themselves, which in turn allows them to lead in their own way. In other words, my definition of leadership makes clear that the aim should be to achieve the best results for the organisation by 'bringing out the best in ourselves and in others'. This means that we want to make use of the full potential of every employee, a goal that many of today's organisations sadly neglect. I have already mentioned that 85% of employees worldwide feel little or no engagement towards the organisations for which they work, so that they have no incentive to make maximum use of their abilities. By bringing out the best in every employee, you develop in them a desire to employ their skills and talents to the best possible effect, by doing the things that they are good at doing. At the same time, this also maximises the likelihood that these employees will influence others to bring out the best in themselves. In other words, this form of leadership is self-reinforcing: leaders do indeed create leaders.

Moreover, the very best leaders surround themselves with others who are best suited to complement their own competencies. Self-insight means that you are not only aware of your strong points and qualities, but also recognise and accept your less good points and qualities. This is by no means easy and it requires courage, especially in today's world where leaders are often expected to have all the answers for everything. Realising that there are some things you do not know and some things you cannot do actually gives you an ideal opportunity to let others shine. Asking for someone's help is not a sign of weakness, but a sign of strength. You are not convinced? Take a look at *The Power of Vulnerability*, the worldwide bestseller by Brené Brown. Nothing gives a person greater satisfaction and a greater sense of being recognised and trusted than the opportunity to use his talents to help someone else at their own request. Making such a request is therefore another way in which you can bring out the best in others and another way in which leaders create leaders.

Letting go

By letting go, it
all gets done. Lao-Tze

Further on in this book I will describe in detail how you can build Positive Connections based on trust, respect, recognition, autonomy and purpose. However, at this point I first need to communicate a message that some of my readers might find 'sensitive': Positive Connection means that you will need to let go more and more. Connecting and letting go? This may sound paradoxical, but it isn't. The fact that trust and autonomy have already been mentioned as two of the basic components of Positive Connection should have given you a clue. Even so, for many leaders, myself included, this obligation to let go of your people can be difficult and challenging. Being in control is something that makes us feel good. Even if that control is largely illusory (which it often is), the idea of being in control of the situation brings many of the leaders I know a sense of calm and reassurance. Again, it is something I also recognise in myself. So watch out that you do not fall into the same trap: forewarned is forearmed! Perhaps you can learn a lesson from the following anecdote. A manager once asked one of my colleagues: 'Is everything under control?' To which my colleague replied: 'Everything? No, because that is impossible. But most things? Yes.'

GUIDING PRINCIPLE 1
POSITIVE CONNECTION

Introduction

We have defined leadership as 'a process of self-insight and positive influencing with the aim of bringing out the best in yourself and in others, in order to achieve the objectives of the organisation'. Positive influencing means that your attitude, actions and words positively influence the attitude, actions and words of others, and vice versa. But if there is no connection between you, this mutual influencing will not be possible. Without a connection, no leadership model or leadership approach can hope to be successful. You can compare it with a smartphone: if you don't have a connection, you can't contact anyone or anything. In short, it is useless.

The stronger your connection, the greater your influence has the potential to be. Yet even more important than the strength of the connection is the nature of the connection. For maximum effect, it must be a Positive Connection that brings people closer together and not a negative connection that drives people apart. In The Leadership Connection, we are searching for the first of these connections, the Positive Connection that strengthens your ties with your colleagues in your common pursuit of the mission and the objectives of your organisation.

Sadly, negative connections have the opposite effect. People are more likely to be repelled, consciously or unconsciously, by others. This can result in resistance and even obstruction. Fortunately, these problems are not insurmountable. Resistance means that energy and engagement are still present, so that resistance, with the right approach, can always be turned around. It is much worse when people disconnect from each other and only do the absolute minimum to get along, which is known in the jargon as presenteeism. In some cases, this inability to connect can lead to resignation, which is the ultimate form of disconnection. Relations that are based purely on power and the fear that it can engender are the classic example of this kind of negative connection, which is something that we still see far too frequently in many organisations. For many years, managers have 'ruled' such organisations in this high-handed manner. Happily, the current scarcity of talent means that employees no longer have to put up with this kind of treatment, since there are now plenty of opportunities to find better forms of leadership elsewhere.

In some people, the idea of 'influencing' evokes a negative image. It almost suggests a kind of manipulation. However, in my opinion there is a huge difference between manipulating someone and positively influencing them. Positive influencing means that you take account of the best interests of the other person and seek to build on their strengths, with the ultimate objective of not only achieving the results the organisation desires but also of improving the work satisfaction of the person concerned. In contrast, manipulation means pushing a person in a specific direction, irrespective of whether or not they wish to travel in that direction and irrespective of whether or not they will benefit or feel happy as a result.

In The Leadership Connection we seek to achieve strong, positive and constructive working relationships based on trust, respect, recognition, autonomy and purpose. For me, these are the five core components of Positive Connection. In the following sections, we will look at the make-up of these components, based on my own practical experience and the input of others who have considered these same themes. It is for each of you to identify the elements that are most important for you and for the people you work with. In this way, you can progressively construct Positive Connections with your colleagues, team members, other employees and leaders that are based on the elements that are relevant for all of you. This is often a process of trial and error, but you will get there in the end and I guarantee that you will be well rewarded for the effort. Why? Because Positive Connections are the key to both excellent business results and optimum happiness at work.

Even so, a word of warning is necessary. Although the five basic components strengthen positive relationships, as you can see in the diagram below, you need to be aware that 'too much' of a specific component is not a good thing. This does not happen very often, but when it does it can have negative rather than positive consequences. For this reason, each section on the individual components will highlight a potential pitfall that may occur if you focus too heavily on that particular component.

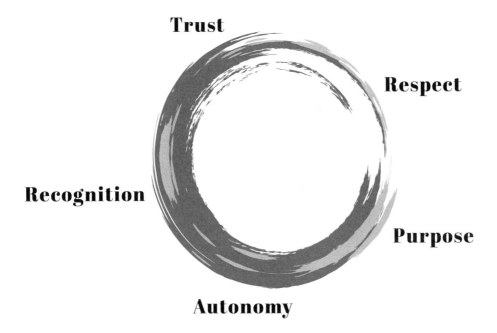

Trust

**He who does
not trust enough will not
be *trusted*.** Lao-Tze

Trust is the most important component for creating connections through which people are prepared to allow their attitudes, actions and/or words to be influenced by someone else. Would you be prepared to follow someone you do not trust?

There is an old Flemish proverb which says that: 'Trust comes on foot, but goes on a horse'. In other words, it often takes time to build up trust, but this trust can be destroyed in an instant if it is abused. Trust consists of a number of elements. Here I will concentrate on trust in the context of an organisation, which is slightly different from trust in a private context. Although the two have similarities (as we shall see presently), 'being competent' plays a less important role in private relationships. In contrast, in an organisational context competence is a crucial factor in persuading you to trust and follow someone else. At the same time, it is important to realise that trust can be given for some competencies and not for others. For example, I trust my IT colleague to repair my computer, but not to inject me with my annual flu vaccination. (Likewise, I would never let the company doctor anywhere near my computer!) Trust in organisations is therefore competence-related. If I am convinced that someone is competent in a particular domain, I will be prepared to follow him in that domain, but not necessarily elsewhere. What's more, trust in someone's confidence can also be conditional. If I am going into hospital for an operation, I unconditionally trust the senior surgeon to perform it. But if I hear that the assistant surgeon is going to perform it, I will only give my permission on condition that the senior surgeon supervises the proceedings.

As far as trust in work relationships is concerned, the following components are, in my opinion, the most important:

Honesty and integrity

> **Trust** is built on telling
> the ***truth***, not telling people
> what they want to ***hear***. Simon Sinek

This may sound like stating the obvious, but honesty and integrity are the foundations on which any relationship of trust is built. Honesty means that you always tell people what needs to be said, so that they always know what is happening and are under no illusions about the position they are in. This in turn means, amongst other things, that you need to communicate difficult messages in a frank and forthright manner, without attempting to embellish the truth. This takes courage. Integrity means that you respect the applicable values and norms in your organisation, your profession and your relations with others. For example, you never reveal information that has been given to you confidentially. Integrity and honesty also mean that you take full responsibility for your mistakes.

Ten questions for reflection on honesty and integrity

- Do you express your opinions freely to others?
- Do people always know where they stand with you?
- Do you hold yourself responsible for all your words and actions?
- Do you explain matters, including your own actions, the way they really are?
- Do you allow others to get the credit for the good work they have done?
- If things go wrong, are you prepared to examine your own part in this failure?
- Do you admit to your mistakes? Even when no one has noticed them?
- Do you follow the rules and honour agreements?
- Do you avoid telling 'white lies'?
- Do you maintain your values and principles, even when put under serious pressure?

Pitfall

You might wonder if we can demonstrate too much honesty and integrity. As far as honesty is concerned, I think that you can indeed 'overdo' it. Honesty does not mean saying everything you think. It would indeed be disconcerting if we all said everything in our thoughts on every occasion! No, honesty means saying what needs to be said in a tactful manner in response to the prevailing situation, on the assumption that your honesty will ultimately improve that situation. Unless you bear in mind the context, your unfiltered comments may come across as being blunt and tactless. That is the 'honesty' pitfall.

The 'integrity' pitfall is more difficult to put into words. It might be described as a kind of excessively principled rigidity that results in you missing important opportunities or prevents you from acting strategically. In this respect, integrity always remains a personal decision; it is up to each person in each situation to decide whether or not there is sufficient justification for bending (but never breaking!) certain values and/or principles.

Being consistent

Trust is built with *consistency.* Lincoln Chafee

In the first instance, I interpret 'being consistent' to mean 'doing what you say you will do'. There are two ways of looking at this: one does indeed involve turning your words into actions; the other involves doing yourself what you ask and expect others to do. The first essentially means 'keeping your word'; the second means 'setting a good example'. However, I like to take the idea of being consistent a stage further by turning it around, so that you not only do what you say, but also say what you intend to do; in other words, you keep people properly informed of your plans, so that they are not unexpectedly surprised by the things you do, which could in some situations lead to negative consequences. Negative surprises are always damaging for trust, which further implies that open, honest and timely communication and feedback are also part of this component. Last but not least, consistency also implies a degree of predictability, so that people know you will react in the same way when the same or similar circumstances repeat themselves.

Ten questions for reflection on being consistent
- Do you do what you say or promise?
- If you are unable to keep a promise, do you tell people?
- If you plan to do something that will have an impact on others, do you tell them?
- Do your actions match your words?
- Do you demonstrate the behaviour that you expect from others?
- Do you react in similar situations in the same way?
- Do you stick to your principles and ideas, even if this makes your work more difficult?
- Do you avoid contradicting yourself?
- Do you avoid constantly changing your opinions and/or decisions?
- Are you predictable in your actions and reactions?

Pitfall

The pitfall of being too consistent is connected to the possible risk of excessive rigidity, which results in a lack of flexibility. At the same time, the rapidly changing context of the modern business environment means that you will not always be able to implement your plans in the way you had intended, so that you may be forced to change direction unexpectedly. For this reason, it is important not to create unrealistic expectations among your people. In this sense, preparing them for the possibility of future change is also a part of being consistent. If, for whatever reason, you are planning to change your attitude, direction or approach, make sure that you clearly inform the people likely to be affected by that change in advance. But avoid becoming someone who 'changes with the wind'; constant changes of direction are seldom appreciated. In contrast, flexibly mapping out and steering a course through the troubled waters of our VUCA world is a sign of good leadership. But make sure you don't overdo it.

Taking account of the interests of others

> We can't **trust** someone *fully* unless we truly know they *care* for us. Aneil & Karen Mishra

Quite rightly, people only trust us when they are convinced that we have their best interests at heart. This means we need to have a knowledge of their needs, wishes and concerns, and must do our best to respond to them positively. How do you acquire this crucial knowledge? There is only one way: by asking them and taking the time to listen carefully and sincerely to what they say. Of course, I realise that it is impossible to always take 100% account of everyone in all circumstances, but if you wish to secure people's trust you must be able to convince them that you have a positive intention to defend their interests to the best of your ability. If your efforts in this respect are not successful, you must always explain to them why this was not possible. This, too, is an inherent part of trust.

Ten questions for reflection on taking account of the interests of others

- Do you know what things are important to others? In terms of approach? In terms of results?
- Do you know how others view a situation?
- Do you know what things are worrying or concerning others?
- Are you aware of the (professional) ambitions and objectives of others?
- Do you show that you are aware of the interests of others?
- Do you genuinely try to take account of the interests of others?
- Do you actively defend the interests of others, even when they are not there?
- Do you try to achieve a balanced consensus between the different interests of others?
- Can you put your own interests to one side for the general good?
- Are you open with others if you decide to act against their interests?

Pitfall

There are two possible aspects to the pitfall of taking too much account of the interests of others. The first is that you try too hard to please these others, in an effort to gain their recognition and approval. Pushing yourself into the background in this manner is often a sign of a lack of self-confidence and self-respect and there is a serious risk that you (and your performance) will ultimately suffer as a result of the neglect of your own interests. The other related risk is that by constantly trying to please everyone, you end up changing direction almost all the time, which can be damaging for your credibility. Without credibility and without self-respect it will be impossible for you to influence people positively.

Competence

Trust is equal parts *character* and *competence*. Stephen Covey

In an organisational context, people will only trust you if they feel that you know what you are doing. But this does not mean that you need to know everything and must always have all the answers. However, it does mean that you will need to understand the questions that people ask and must also have the wisdom to know where you can find the knowledge and information you need to formulate the right answers and decisions. In other words, competence is not only about being aware of what you know and what you are able to do, but also about being aware of what you do not know and what you cannot do, so that you can go in search of the necessary advice. This means that in some circumstances you might only give trust or gain trust for the implementation of specific tasks where the necessary degree of competence is clearly present, but not for other tasks where the required level of competence is currently still lacking.

Ten questions for reflection on competence
- Do you have a realistic view of your talents, shortcomings and points for development?
- Do you ask for feedback from others about your talents, shortcomings and points for development?
- Do you avoid presenting yourself to others as being more competent than you really are?
- If there is something you cannot do or do not know, do you admit this freely to others?
- If there is something you cannot do or do not know, do you ask for help from others?
- Do you invest in all the competencies you need for your work?
- Do you surround yourself with people who can compensate for your weaker competencies?

- Can you accept that others are sometimes better at some things than you are?
- Do you seek assistance if you lack the competencies for a particular task?
- If you have doubts, do you ask for a second opinion?

Pitfall

It is difficult for a person to be too competent! No, the pitfall with competencies is that you stick too rigidly to the competencies you already have. If you want to learn, you have to be prepared to step out of your comfort zone and this always involves a certain degree of risk. This is not a problem, providing you do it consciously, assessing the risks accurately in advance and taking measures to keep them within repairable limits. Having someone to whom you can turn for support and advice, when necessary, is also a good idea. In contrast, refusing to move away from the things you currently know may make you risk-averse, so that you end up missing crucial opportunities to learn — and learning is essential in our rapidly changing world. For this reason, it makes sense from time to time to accept tasks with which you are not yet 100% familiar and therefore not 100% comfortable.

I was a mentor for Isabelle during her 'first hundred days' in her new job in an environmental organisation. Her task was to coordinate the activities of all the different services that the organisation provides to the government. She was not expected to lead any of these activities, but simply to ensure that the different services took better account of each other and coordinated their actions, where possible. These services are strictly regulated and frequently appear in the news, because the different political parties have widely differing views about the services and the way they are run. Most of the organisation's employees are environmentally aware and strongly committed to improving the natural environment wherever possible. For this reason, they are often of the opinion that they need to apply the regulations relating to their services as strictly as possible and would prefer to see even stricter norms. They believe that the politicians are too lax in this respect.

Isabelle is an enthusiastic and cheerful person, yet also very determined. She does not like beating about the bush and always wants to make progress quickly. As the first step in her hundred-day plan, we discussed how she could get a better picture of the context and the situation in which she now found herself. We identified all the relevant stakeholders and assessed how they might best be approached. Her manager had given her a broad outline of all the various interests that were at play and suggested which of the stakeholders were on the same wavelength and which ones were not. Next, Isabelle and I together drew up a list of all the people she wanted to see. We also prepared a question list that would allow her to extract the maximum amount of information from each of these meetings. But the most important part of the question list was her introduction. In this introduction she explained what she saw as the main purpose of these exploratory conversations: not to take any immediate action, but to gain information that she would view with an open mind.

Planning how she should proceed was no easy task. From the very first day she was deluged with requests for meetings. If she had agreed to all these requests, her agenda would have been full to overflowing. As a result, she took a conscious decision to first make room for her exploratory conversations. Most of the people she approached were keen to take part in these conversations, seeing them as the ideal opportunity to express both their wishes for the future and their displeasure with certain matters from the past. Isabelle noted down everything they had to say: their stories, their ambitions, their frustrations... She finished each conversation with a run-through of the main points, to make sure that she had understood everything correctly. And, most important of all, she underlined that she was not in a position to make any promises at that stage. She first wanted to hear what everyone had to say.

Of course, it was impossible for her to talk in person to all the personnel who were involved in the services provided to the government. However, Isabelle devised a way to get around that. She made space in her busy programme to go on three study trips with three different teams on three different days. This took her to some of the remotest of the organisation's environmental stations and showed her the kinds of challenges with which the staff were confronted every day: bad weather, muddy fields, angry livestock, even angrier farmers... 'Nothing that a pair of wellingtons, some rainproof trousers, a thick overcoat and even thicker skin can't fix,' she told me laughing. This made a strong impression on the organisation's managers and employees alike. In the past, no one had made the effort to do this;

to see how the world looked to the people at the sharp end of the organisation's operations. Even though she was not able to see all the field workers personally, her positive reputation soon spread throughout the organisation. She was steadily winning trust.

By the time she had finished her exploratory conversations, she had a notebook full of people's different opinions, expectations, complaints, wishes, dreams, interests and ambitions. The moment had now arrived for her to draw her conclusions and communicate them. She made a summary of key observations, most of which had been mentioned by various people. She highlighted clearly and honestly the areas where there was already a good deal of agreement and the areas where there was no agreement at all. She was not afraid to tackle 'sacred cows' both inside and outside the organisation, but always did so in a correct manner and without making personal assessments. She made clear to everyone where the future presented opportunities, but also where difficulties were likely to occur. She then communicated her summary to all relevant stakeholders and employees.

The next step in her hundred-day plan was to set up a work group to develop a strategy for the future. Once this had been done, Isabelle again communicated details of the proposed strategy to all relevant stakeholders and employees. She explained how she had arrived at her action plan and specified clearly how it met (or failed to meet) the expectations of certain groups. She was also honest and direct about how the plan would have an impact on everyone concerned. Isabelle knew in advance that not everyone would be happy with what she had to say, but her openness and her honesty won her much credit and, more importantly, trust. This trust, which she had acquired through listening carefully and communicating with clarity, meant that many of the people with whom she would have to work were prepared to compromise on their demands and were willing to contribute to a common strategy more fully than ever before.

Respect

Knowledge will give you *power*, but *character, respect.* Bruce Lee

Respect is related to the importance of values and norms. If someone recognises in your behaviour values and norms that are also important to them, you will earn their respect. In that way, you become a valuable person for them. This is another vital element in the creation of Positive Connections with others, through which your attitude, words and actions influence these others.

Values and norms are first and foremost something personal. We acquire them as a result of our upbringing, education and training. However, our environment, such as the land where we live or the organisation where we work, also helps to determine our values and norms. If it is the norm (as is the case in some countries) that colleagues shake hands when they come into the office each morning, it will be seen as disrespectful if you do not do the same. Of course, this does not mean that you never can or never should go against the values and norms prevailing in an organisation. If everyone always arrives late for the start of meetings and you make an effort to try and get everyone to start on time, this will gain you respect by others who also regard 'starting on time' as an important norm.

How can you work to improve your respect in the eyes of others? Research suggests that this is largely a matter of following the accepted values and norms, combined with the extent to which others are able to appreciate your personal values and norms. That being said, I still believe that it is possible to work at gaining respect. In the following paragraphs I will detail some of the elements that in my opinion lead to greater respect. But the most important element of all is this: doing what you are good at and doing it well. Strong performance, carried out in an exemplary manner, almost always wins respect.

As far as respect in a working relationship is concerned, for me the most important components are as follows:

Respect for yourself

Respect yourself and others will respect you. Confucius

Perhaps it sounds strange, but others will not respect you if you do not respect yourself. Respecting yourself means that you stand up for your own convictions and opinions. It means that you dare to set your own limits and have the courage to say 'no', when necessary. It means making use of your talents and doing the things that you like to do and are good at doing. However, it does not mean that you cannot adjust your style or approach depending on the circumstances, although you should always do this in your own personal manner. Respecting yourself is being true to yourself.

Ten questions for reflection on self-respect
- Do you respect your own values and priorities?
- Do you say 'no' to things that could harm you?
- Do you follow your dreams?
- Do you avoid effacing yourself to comply with the wishes of others?
- Do you avoid being limited by the influence (words and actions) of others?
- Do you regard yourself as being good enough?
- Do you have the courage to tackle the things you want to change?
- Do you treat yourself as well as you treat others?
- Do you stand up for your talent?
- Do you stand up for yourself?

Pitfall

The pitfall of respecting yourself too much is obvious: it will appear to others as a form of egocentrism or even narcissism. If you place yourself at the centre of the world, people will not like it and will lose respect for you. Egocentrism and narcissism lead to extremely unhealthy relationships and certainly do not contribute to Positive Connection. Even so, it is a pitfall with which you may be confronted, especially as you climb the hierarchical management ladder. Perhaps this is not so surprising or illogical. The more your job requires you to express your opinion, the more you are likely to feel that your opinion is the right one — always and everywhere. For this reason, it is important to challenge yourself sufficiently, if you have the privilege of being able to make many decisions in organisations.

Respect for identity and diversity

> **Respect** is *appreciation* for the *identity* of the other, for the way in which he or she is **unique**. Annie Gottlieb

Our diversity as human beings means that no two people have precisely the same values and norms. This gives us two options. We can either concentrate on the things that divide us and become irritated by the fact that some people act according to values and norms that are not ours. Or else we can concentrate on the things that we share and regard the differences as elements that actually enrich the organisation for which we all work. With this second (and clearly better) option, you accept people as they are and attempt to see the added value that their diversity creates. People feel respected if they are allowed to be their true selves and are not expected to fit into pigeon-holes determined by others. It is generally the case in the world of organisations (and beyond) that diverse teams are stronger teams, provided that the team members are prepared to build constructively on each other's diversity. This demands effort and dedication.

Ten questions for reflection on identity and diversity

- Do you respect everyone for who they are?
- Do you respect the values and preferences of others?
- Do you treat everyone the same way?
- Do you search for added value in other opinions, values and preferences?
- Do you take account of the opinions and feelings of others?
- Do you respect other people's boundaries?
- Do you allow people the right to their own opinion, even if you do not agree with it?
- Do you demonstrate support for the values that others possess?
- Do you stand up for others who are unfairly treated?
- If you disagree with someone, do you say this in a respectful manner?

Pitfall

Is it possible to have too much respect for identity and diversity? Yes, it is — if that respect is purely one-sided. Diversity can offer a huge added value to any organisation, if it can fulfil unsatisfied needs and requirements in others. In this way, for example, my lack of creativity can be compensated for by the creativity of my colleague. But identity and diversity can also sometimes lead to a clash with other personal values and/or with the values and norms of the organisation. When this happens, it is necessary for all those involved to find a modus vivendi, a constructive way of dealing with the differences. It is not reasonable or acceptable to expect anyone to completely efface his own identity in favour of someone else's. In this sense, 'mutual' is undoubtedly the most important adjective that should be used in conjunction with 'respect'. Respect must be a two-way street, a matter of give and take.

Courtesy and humility

There is no respect for others without *humility* in yourself. Henri Amiel

In essence, courtesy means showing respect for others through the practical application of good manners and etiquette. Courtesy in all its forms helps you to gain respect. Moreover, as the old proverb puts it: 'Politeness costs you nothing'. Within organisations, you can see courtesy at work in the simplest of things: not interrupting people when they are speaking; not shouting at people; reacting calmly and collectedly in heated situations; not gossiping about people. As you climb higher up the hierarchical ladder, courtesy also increasingly becomes a form of humility: the 'big boss' who pours the coffee when visited by a less senior employee; the head of department who asks the office cleaner how things are going; etc. Courtesy and humility are matters of small details. A title alone will seldom win you genuine respect; on the contrary, the higher you rise in the organisation, the more people will expect of you. In this respect, courtesy is a win from which everyone benefits.

Ten questions for reflection on courtesy and humility

- Do you approach everyone in a friendly manner?
- Do you respect the customs and habits of places where you are a guest?
- Do you thank others for what they do for you?
- Do you respect other people's time?
- Do you offer a genuine apology when you make a mistake?
- Do you refrain from making comments about others behind their back?
- Do you assume that you can still learn something from everyone?
- Do you regard all information as confidential, unless otherwise agreed?
- Do you offer your help to others?
- Do you first try to understand others before expecting them to understand you?

Pitfall

Too much courtesy and humility can lead to submissiveness and an excessive focus on socially desirable behaviour. One important implication of this is that people will not really know where they stand with you. Is what you are saying your real opinion or are you just being polite? This lack of certainty makes it impossible to build Positive Connections. In addition, being too polite and too humble can often come across to others as an act, as something not real. This is what is meant, for example, by the term 'false modesty'; in other words, pretending to be modest in the hope of getting a compliment. This kind of behaviour is often a sign of a lack of self-confidence and self-respect. Moreover, it can often be interpreted by others as being manipulative and it gives most people an uncomfortable feeling. This does not immediately contribute to the making of Positive Connections.

Listening to others and showing interest in their intentions

One of the sincerest forms of respect is actually listening to what *another* has to say. Bryant H. McGill

Even if you are not completely in agreement with what someone is saying or doing, you can still listen to him and attempt to discover his intentions. This is also a form of respect. If you take as your starting point the assumption that everyone acts with good intentions, it is often enough simply to ask the person in question to explain his intentions and how he plans to implement them through his words and actions. As soon as you understand what his intentions are, you can, where necessary, attempt to search together to find a better way to put those intentions into practice. Listening and showing interest are important keys to respect.

Ten questions for reflection on listening and showing interest
- If you listen to someone, do you listen with your full attention?
- Do you look for the good intentions behind the words and actions of others?
- Are you curious about the opinions and motivations of others?
- Do you wait until you understand the intentions of others before you react?
- Do you search for the origins and background of other people's intentions?
- Can you put your preconceptions to one side?
- Do you try to put yourself in the position of the other person?
- Are you aware that no one — not even you — has a monopoly on the truth?
- Can you show understanding for unintentional mistakes?
- Do you help others to express and realise their intentions in the best possible way?

Pitfall

Listening to others and showing interest in their intentions is one of the most important components for developing mutual respect and is therefore a crucial aspect for building Positive Connections. The biggest problem in this regard is time, which is an increasingly scarce commodity in every organisation. Listening takes time. Too much listening to one person and his intentions may therefore mean that there is no time for another person's intentions to be discussed. Or, even worse, for your own intentions to be discussed. If this is a deliberate ploy – so that you do not need to defend your own position – too much listening to others and showing interest in their intentions degenerates into a lack of assertiveness in putting forward your own opinions and intentions. This is known as being sub-assertive. Another related problem is the tendency to allow too much time for the discussion of intentions that are most similar to our own.

> *A new water pipe is being laid in our street. From my office, I have a fine view of the collaboration between the different contractors. Everyone in the street is happy with the approach they have taken to the work. Disruption has been kept to a minimum: the 'no parking' areas are clearly indicated, the entrances to garages and front doors have been kept free, the pavements are swept regularly, and we always get a friendly 'good morning' from the workers when we pass.*
>
> *My personal curiosity prompts me to go in search of the team leader. But it is not immediately clear who he is. No one is wearing different clothes or a different helmet. No one is walking around with plans in his hands or issuing instructions. No one is an obvious point of contact for the neighbours, and no one seems to be checking the work.*
>
> *After a time, I finally notice that there is one person who is different from the rest; a fairly young man who is doing lots of different tasks. He brings a new supply of paving stones when the existing supply has almost run out. He helps if the new pipes need to be manoeuvred through the parked cars. He sweeps the street as soon as there is too much mud. He assists the crane driver to repair a technical defect. In short, he intervenes wherever it is necessary to allow the team to continue doing its work effectively. He is usually the first person to arrive on site in the morning and*

the last person to leave at night, having first made sure that everything has been tidied up properly.

Even at a distance, you can see that he is highly respected by his team members. They are not afraid to ask him questions, because they know that he will always be ready to provide them with the necessary advice and, above all, action. It is also inspiring to see how he treats all his team members with equal respect, irrespective of the tasks they perform, irrespective of their origins and their knowledge of the local language (it is clearly a multinational team with representatives from half of Europe!), and irrespective of the moment when they approach him. He radiates an energy, a pride in his job and a friendliness that are infectious.

I have the impression that he uses his team members to do the tasks that they most like doing and therefore do well. Those who like to do the same tasks over and over again, like the men who re-lay the pavements, are allowed to do so. Those that like variety – first some digging, next a bit of pipe laying, then filling in the trench, etc. – also seem to get what they want.

The collaboration between the different parts of the team reminds me of an orchestra. Everyone works together in the same serene, calm and efficient manner, with all the different tasks and skills finely attuned to each other. The only difference is that the conductor does not stand at the front, but is constantly moving around between his 'musicians'! He knows all the scores and all the instruments, and intervenes wherever he is needed to achieve the end result that everyone wants. And he does it day after day.

This is the kind of leadership I look up to and for which I have the deepest respect. If I was able to record what I can see from my office window on camera, I would have material that I would be able to show at the highest hierarchical levels as an example of what real leadership looks like.

To show our appreciation for the way the work in our street was carried out by this team, we sent (with pleasure) a congratulatory e-mail to the contractor's office. We didn't really expect an answer, but the very next day we got an e-mail in reply from the engineer who had been in charge. He said that he was delighted to get such positive feedback and promised to pass on our kind words to every member of his team. It is clear that good leadership is well anchored in this organisation. Or how exemplary behaviour can have an infectious and motivating effect that sends organisations into a positive upwards spiral.

Recognition

> **Leaders** don't look for *recognition* from others, leaders look for **others** to *recognise.* Simon Sinek

If you want to create strong connections with your colleagues, it is important that you know who they are. You need to be aware of the role they play and the results they achieve. This, in a nutshell, is what recognition means: existing as a valuable person in the eyes of others. No one likes to be ignored or treated as a number. Everyone knows the feeling of wanting to be seen and to be regarded not as a cog in a machine, but as a competent person with a passion for their work.

Recognition in a classic organisation is often immediately associated with remuneration and rewards. In my opinion, these are 'cold' forms of recognition. Studies have repeatedly shown that money seldom gives people the recognition they crave. On the contrary, some research suggests that paying people more for the execution of knowledge-intensive tasks actually diminishes their level of recognition, motivation and satisfaction.

I prefer 'warm' forms of recognition. One of the warmest is when people ask for your advice or specifically ask you to carry out a particular task. This is the clearest possible evidence that what you do and how you do it are recognised and valued by others. Likewise, an expression of personal appreciation from someone for work that you have carried out is another important aspect of recognition. Viewed in these terms, recognition is not just recognition for what you do; it is also recognition for who you are. Giving and receiving recognition helps to promote connection.

As far as recognition in a working relationship is concerned, for me the most important components are as follows:

Knowing

> **I am not interested in how people *move*, but in what *moves* them.** Pina Bausch

If you want to give recognition to someone else, you first need to know that person, so that you can know what will make them feel recognised. Because this book is about leadership in organisations, this means knowing others in an organisational context. In other words, what is important for these others in their work environment? You can get to know others better by asking them questions and listening to their answers, but you can probably learn just as much by simply observing them. The common factor for successfully using both these methods is the need to pay attention to and have genuine interest in the other person. How does he approach his work? How does he deal with his colleagues? People's words and actions will often allow you to deduce what things are important to them and what things less so.

Ten questions for reflection on knowing
- Do you know the (professional) ambitions of others in your organisation?
- Do you know how others want to make a difference?
- Do you know which talents others want to expand?
- Do you know which points for development others wish to work at improving?
- Do you know how others prefer to work?
- Do you know which kinds of tasks and activities others most like doing?
- Do you know which kinds of tasks and activities others least like doing?

- Do you know what values are important to others?
- Do you know what convictions others hold?
- Do you know what practical priorities others have?

Pitfall

Can you know the other person too well? To be honest, this is one of the few components of Positive Connection where it is not really possible to take things too far. But this does not mean that there are no potential pitfalls to having such knowledge. The first possible pitfall is the way you acquire that knowledge: your interest in others has to be genuine and not pretended. If people discover your interest is false, this will destroy rather than promote Positive Connection. One sincere question is better than ten fake ones. In a similar way, we sometimes go in search of knowledge about the other person out of a sense of curiosity (often sensation-inspired), so that we can discover things that he might actually prefer to keep to himself. This, again, is not a form of genuine interest. Last but not least, knowing someone too well often leads us to make assumptions about how the other person thinks and acts. In this way, we have a tendency to decide things for him – what he wants, what he is interested in, etc. – rather than letting him decide for himself.

Recognising

Attention is the *rarest* and *purest* form of generosity. Simone Weil

As you get to know others better, you will be able to recognise when they have done something that is important to them. Recognising things in this way requires you to pay a great deal of attention to what your colleagues do and to the things that interest them. In this context, it is not only the result that is important, but also (and more often) the way the result is achieved. In fact, I would go further: even if there is no result or the undertaking is a failure, it is still possible to recognise what people have done and give them due recognition for it, providing they have made a serious and worthwhile effort. In this way, you can acknowledge their commitment, their approach and even the way they cope with failure.

Ten questions for reflection on recognising

- Do you pay enough attention to the work of others?
- Do you notice the things to which others devote either a great deal or very little attention?
- When people are talking about their work, do you hear what they are really saying?
- When people are talking to and about each other, do you hear what they are really saying?
- When internal/external customers are talking about others, do you hear what they are really saying?
- Do you notice what kinds of tasks others like to accept?
- Do you notice how others approach their work?
- Do you notice which new skills others are keen to learn and how they go about this?
- Do you notice which activities others are less good at?
- Do you notice which activities others avoid?

Pitfall

Recognising can be taken to extremes in two different ways: by primarily (or even exclusively) recognising good things or, conversely, by primarily (or even exclusively) recognising bad things. Both can be the result of what we generally refer to as a self-fulfilling prophecy. Consciously or subconsciously, we want to see the other succeed or fail, and therefore we recognise what we expect to recognise. However, there are also other factors that can prevent us from recognising in a balanced way. For example, it is always easier and more pleasant to recognise (and give recognition for) positive things. Alternatively, so-called negativity bias means that on many occasions it is the negative things that strike us most. In other words, the most important pitfall in this context is the danger of reaching subjectively positive or subjectively negative conclusions. For this reason, it is always a good idea for you to listen to how others observe and assess the person in question. Different opinions bring us closer to objectivity.

Appreciating

Appreciation is a wonderful thing. It makes what is *excellent* in others belong to us as well. Voltaire

For me, appreciating means showing that you value and esteem what is important to others. This display of appreciation should not be confined to moments when important results have been achieved. You can appreciate what others do at any time, even, for example, if an action has failed, notwithstanding the tremendous effort that everyone has made. In this sense, appreciation not only values what people do, but also (and primarily) who they are. It therefore serves to highlight and praise people's good qualities. Nothing creates a better connection than for people to feel that they are seen, recognised and appreciated as being an added value for the organisation as a whole.

Ten questions for reflecting on appreciating

- Do you compliment others about their work, results and approach?
- Do you explain to others what you regard as the strengths of their approach?
- Do you explain to others how their work has made a difference (to you)?
- Do you explain to others what is original, creative and unique in their approach?
- Do you explain to others how they can build further on their talents?
- Do you compliment others about the positive way they deal with setbacks?
- Do you compliment others when they acquire new competencies?
- Do you compliment others when they move out of their comfort zone?
- Do you ask others to help you (or other people) with the activities in which they excel?
- Do you appreciate others for who they are and what they mean to you?

Pitfall

Although there are many organisations where too little appreciation is shown, it is also possible to show too much. The biggest pitfall you need to avoid is that your appreciation is not regarded as being sincere and genuine by those for whom it is intended. This can happen if the appreciation you give is out of all proportion to the action or personal quality that you want to recognise. Exaggerated appreciation is seldom seen as being credible and can even embarrass the recipient in front of his colleagues. This will never contribute towards making a Positive Connection. In this context, you need to bear in mind that some people very quickly see appreciation as being exaggerated. For example, if they regard a particular task as part of their standard task package, they see no reason why they should be recognised or praised for doing it: 'After all, that's what I'm paid for,' they often comment. That being said, with most people it is still a good idea to occasionally show that you appreciate what they do, even for routine tasks.

▶ *Marie is a young engineering student at university. This year she has taken on a role as the leader of one of the student teams at the university. These student teams work on the development of advanced and pioneering technology, in competition with other universities. Marie has opted to work on the Strong Wind project, a wind turbine that will produce significantly more electricity, thanks to the use of a revolutionary new generator. The team has a year to develop the most efficient version of this generator, which will then be judged in a competition in Singapore against rival projects from some of the best universities in the world. Together with the senior engineer, Cathleen, and the planning and finance controller, Jens, Marie is a member of the management team that will be responsible for a group of more than forty students who have agreed to take part in the project voluntarily.*

During a first meeting, Cathleen, Jens and Marie discuss how they will divide up their responsibilities. They agree that Marie will focus primarily on two key areas: external relations and internal team relations. This latter aspect involves all matters dealing with the collaboration, motivation and well-being of the team. This is an important task, because the pressure to perform well in the competition is huge. All the team members are enthusiastically determined to defend the honour and reputation of their university. So determined, in fact, that there is a risk of burn-out, because this is what has happened on more than one occasion during similar competitions in the past.

After a successful weekend getting to know each other, the team starts work on the design of their generator. This is the moment for Marie to start what she calls her 'little walks'. She takes each member of the team individually for a stroll though the nearby university park, so that she can get to know them better. She wants to learn more about their motivation, their expectations, their concerns, what contribution they would like to make, how they would like to make it, etc. For Marie, this is also the ideal opportunity to explain her role and intentions. Above all, she emphasises that they can always come to her if they find that they are experiencing problems.

After five months, it becomes clear that the competition in Singapore will not take place, because the main sponsor is in financial difficulties and has had to pull out. This is a major disappointment for the team: what was expected to be the highlight of their year on the project has been snatched from their grasp. This is where

Marie's little walks prove their value. She listens carefully and sympathetically to the frustration of the team members and learns from them what they want to do next. On the basis of this input, the management team decides that they will organise their own record-breaking attempt for the performance of the new generator. During her subsequent walks, Marie soon picks up that this new objective has rekindled the team's motivation.

A few weeks later, the generator produces electricity using wind energy for the very first time. It is an important and unforgettable moment. Next morning, Marie brings in croissants and buns for a celebratory breakfast. It is a small gesture, but it gives a huge boost to the team. But then the COVID crisis breaks out, bringing new disappointment. From now on, the team can only work in groups of three in the workshop, which means that at times they need to work day and night to give everyone the necessary workshop time. Marie's little walks are now replaced by video chats. The progress and challenges of the individual team members are shared online, so that everyone can follow everything that is happening and get their own chance to be 'in the spotlight'. In this way, the progress and challenges of the individuals become the progress and challenges of the team as a whole. Everyone feels involved.

The day for the record-breaking attempt finally arrives. There is enough wind and the team's many supporters and sympathisers can follow the event via a livestream. The generator systematically produces more and more power as the brakes are progressively released. Everything seems to be going well until the emergency brake self-activates and shuts down the turbine. Even so, a quick check of the figures shows that the amount of electricity already generated has broken the record: sadly, not the world record, but at least the record for their own university. The team members experience a curious mixture of happiness and disappointment, and they all need to find a way to come to terms with what they are feeling. There is still reason to celebrate: the fact that everyone has given the best of himself/herself; the fact that they have all shared a fascinating and enriching experience; the fact that they have all made new friends; the fact that they all had the determination to make it to the finishing lines, notwithstanding all the setbacks they encountered along the way. But the finest form of appreciation came in the shape of a documentary made by the university about 'their' Strong Wind year, in which everyone appeared and was allowed to have their own say. A unique souvenir of a unique project.

Autonomy

Control leads to *compliance,* autonomy leads to *engagement.* Daniel H. Pink

I define autonomy as 'the extent to which you have control over how, when, where and with whom you work'. Research has shown that the possession of a certain degree of autonomy improves intrinsic motivation. Projects, objectives, tasks and activities that we are able to decide for ourselves give a boost to our drive and to our work satisfaction. In other words, autonomy provides a double win.

Autonomy determines, as it were, the tightness of the connection between two employees. Unlimited autonomy means that there is no connection whatsoever. Limited autonomy (especially very limited autonomy) means that the connection risks becoming oppressive. Do you remember the images of Charlie Chaplin in the film *Modern Times*, where his only task is to fasten two bolts in keeping with the rhythm set by a machine? That is how soul-destroying a lack of autonomy can sometimes be.

But the most counterproductive form of autonomy is unclear autonomy, when the employees do not really know what they are allowed to say, do and decide for themselves. This can lead to endless misunderstandings, frustrations and poor results. It is a situation that still frequently occurs, because there are many organisations where too little attention is paid to making clear agreements on autonomy and fail to set clear agreements about how it can be implemented.

As far as autonomy in a working relationship is concerned, for me the most important components are as follows:

The playing field and the rules

Confidence without *clarity* is a disaster. Sadhguru

Nobody would ever consider taking up a new sport without first obtaining clear information about the nature of the playing field and the rules of the game. Even for a relatively simple 'sport' like a family game of beach volleyball you still need to improvise a net and use your flip-flops to mark out the area of the 'court', so that you can determine whether the ball is 'in' or 'out'. However, it is amazing how many organisations still fail to respect this basic preparatory procedure. Time after time, employees are left in the dark about how far they can go, what decisions they can take, what contacts they can make and what activities they can/must carry out. There is too little discussion on the 'rules' that we need and want others to follow. What are the minimal procedures that need to be respected, how and when do other stakeholders need to become involved, who decides how the work should be carried out, etc.? These are not complex matters but failure to address them can result in a huge waste of time and effort, as well as generating unnecessary frustration and demotivation. Making clear agreements is the key to success. True, this also requires the investment of additional time and effort at the beginning of a project or task, but you will more than win back that time and effort during the implementation.

Ten questions for reflecting on the playing field and the rules
- Are you able to decide for yourself the amount of autonomy you would like to have?
- Do you ask others about the amount of autonomy they would like to have?
- Do you stand up for your own wishes with regard to autonomy and your preferred approach?
- Do you take account of the wishes of others with regard to autonomy and their preferred approach?
- Do you make clear agreements in advance about autonomy and the approach to be used?

- Do you ensure that your autonomy and approach are in keeping with your competencies and/or the competencies of others?
- Do you know how far you can go when it comes to making independent decisions?
- Do you know and always respect the (minimum) rules and procedures that need to be followed?
- Do you consult with others (leaders, colleagues, etc.) if there is doubt or uncertainty about autonomy and the approach to be taken?
- Do you dare to ask others for more autonomy if you have a need for it?

Pitfall

If you take things too far when defining the playing field and setting the rules, this can lead to inertia and slow performance. It is very difficult at the start of a project or task to envisage all the possible situations that may arise and to decide in each of these situations how much autonomy you should give to the people involved. You need to concentrate on setting broad guidelines; otherwise you risk wasting too much time. In this respect, it is a good idea to apply the Pareto rule. If you focus on the 20% of situations that are likely to occur most frequently, you will cover autonomy issues for 80% of the project. The remaining 20% of issues can be decided as the project progresses. All your decisions should take account of the culture and expectations within your organisation. Some organisations adopt a 'do now, apologise later' approach, whereas others expect employees to seek permission before they initiate new action.

Control versus letting go

> # Knowledge is *learning* something every day. Wisdom is *letting go* of something every day. Zen proverb

When you are determining levels of autonomy with your colleagues, it is important to enter into agreements that everyone feels comfortable with. If you set someone a task, be honest and clear with yourself and with them about how you want the task to be carried out. If possible, try to have the courage to 'let go'. Think about the skills the person possesses and about the possible risks resulting from failure. Having balanced these factors, decide upon a level of autonomy that is acceptable to you. But before implementing this decision, first discuss your proposal with the person concerned, to ensure that this level is also acceptable to him. This is the moment when you need to define together the playing field and the rules to achieve autonomy that everyone can live with, respecting the other person's need for control.

Ten questions for reflection on control versus letting go
- Do you know and recognise your own need for control?
- Do you dare to stand up for your own need for control?
- Do you question your own need for control?
- Do you adjust your need for control to reflect the needs of others for autonomy?
- Do you adjust your need for control to reflect the competencies of others?
- Do you seriously consider and weigh the advantages of control against the advantages of letting go?
- Do you check how your control appears to others?
- Do you take the risk of allowing (correctable) mistakes by being more willing to let go?
- Can you accept that tasks are carried out in ways other than the ones you prefer?
- Can you defend other people's ways of working, even if they are not your own?

Pitfall

The pitfalls of too much control and too much letting go are perhaps the most obvious of all. Too much control leads to excessive interference in what others do and suffocates any relationship. This is hardly the best way to build Positive Connections! Too much letting go can also be tempting, because by giving people full autonomy you can neatly avoid you own responsibilities for the work or project in question. In addition, it also saves you a lot of valuable time. Of course, there is an obvious danger that your people will feel unsupported and disappointed at what they will see as your lack of interest in what they are doing. In other words, finding the right levels of control and letting go is a constant balancing act, in which you can only be successful through consultation with the others involved.

The safety net

To stand up for yourself takes strength, but to stand up for others takes *courage*. Alice Ann Jennet Lisenby

No matter how much or how little autonomy you give to others, you always need to make sure that they have a safety net. Swimming in deep water for the first time can be exciting, but it is not without risk. If people know that there is a lifeline to pull them out if they get into difficulties, this will make it easier for them to have the confidence they need to go their own way. In organisational terms, this means that there needs to be an experienced person close at hand to whom they can turn, if the circumstances require it. Not someone to constantly check in detail how the work is progressing, but someone who occasionally asks if there is anything he can do to help. This is another constant balancing act: you need to make clear to your people that you have confidence in them to get the job done, whilst at the same time letting them know that you are there, should the need arise.

Ten questions for reflecting on the safety net
- Are you available to others if they need you?
- If you are not available, do you provide another source of help they can turn to?
- Is it clear to others that they can turn to you or someone else for support?
- Do your people have the courage to come to you for help, even if they have made a (serious) mistake?
- Do you compliment others if they ask for support at the right moment?
- If your people ask for support, do you turn this into a learning moment?
- Do you try to develop the self-confidence of others?
- Do you try to give your people the maximum amount of independence?
- Do you stand up for others when they have made (accidental) mistakes?
- Do you motivate your people to be a safety net for each other?

Pitfall

The pitfalls of a safety net are twofold. If the net is too obvious and comes into action too soon, it risks making things too easy for your people. As a result, they fail to concentrate and make the necessary effort that is required to succeed. They know that everything is covered and that solutions for any problems will always be found. So why bother? The other risk is that when someone eventually falls into your safety net, you are inclined to take over the whole show, rather than helping him to his feet (although not necessarily straight back up to the tightrope at the very top of the tent!). Overreacting in this way can undermine people's confidence and self-reliance. The purpose of a safety net is to avoid critical incidents in which people can suffer – literally or figuratively – irreparable harm. At the same time, it is also intended to give people the chance to learn in a safe manner. So even if you do feel obliged to take over after someone has fallen into your net, at least do it together with that person, so that he can continue to learn.

Mike is searching in a dark beer cellar to find the connection for the tap installation in the bar upstairs. Today marks the end of his second month on the road accompanied by Peter, one of the brewery's more experienced technicians. Peter has been travelling throughout Belgium for more than 25 years now, installing and maintaining pipe systems for draught beer and other drinks. It is highly specialised work, much more than people might think. If you want good beer to come out of your taps (and let's face it: who doesn't!), temperature, carbon dioxide levels, pressure and flow all play a crucial role. The ultimate test, of course, is how the beer tastes. You can compare this to an aroma specialist mixing a new perfume or a coffee roaster selecting the right blend of beans. Peter's curved belly suggests that he has had plenty of practical experience when it comes to sampling beers. After all, he has to make sure that they are all perfectly in order, doesn't he? Peter's colleagues regard him as the specialist amongst the brewery's workforce. If anyone has a flavour problem they can't solve, they know that Peter will have the answer.

Mike joined the brewery six months ago as a young technician. Initially, he was sent on the road with another experienced technician, so that he could learn the tricks of the trade, but this did not go well. The technician hardly allowed him to do any of the actual work and seemed happy to use Mike as a porter all the necessary tools to and from the van. Mike had assumed that he would be given the chance to do some of the installation work himself – how on earth could he be expected to learn otherwise? – but his colleague always found some excuse for doing it himself: it was too difficult, there wasn't much time, the customer had insisted, etc. After four months of this, Mike had had enough and was on the point of resigning. As a last resort, he discussed the problem with his section manager – and the manager decided to put him with Peter.

Once he was on the road with Peter, things went much better for Mike. Whenever they entered a pub or hotel, Peter always asked Mike: 'So what do we need to do here?' Mike then explained the tasks he thought needed to be carried out and how he would do them, if it was left up to him. Mike was actually turning out to be quite a good technician, so if what he said was right, Peter let him get on with it, although he was always there to give advice or lend a helping hand, should it be necessary. Sometimes Peter queried why Mike wanted to do particular tasks in a particular way and they would then discuss if there might not be a better way. But in the end it was usually Mike who was allowed to decide. If, as an outsider, you watched the two of them working together, you might have been forgiven for thinking that it was Mike who was the experienced technician and Peter who was the learner! It was Mike who made all the technical decisions, with Peter just assisting with the implementation. Occasionally, Mike still asked Peter for a bit of advice. To which the older man usually replied: 'Well, what do you think?'

Mike is delighted to have Peter as a colleague. He feels that he is learning all the time and appreciates that someone as experienced as Peter is willing to share all his knowledge with the 'newcomer'. For his part, Peter also enjoys passing on everything he has learnt over the years and is pleased that Mike seems to have the same passion for the job. He knows by now that Mike will usually make the right decisions, although things still occasionally go wrong. One day Mike opened the wrong tap by mistake, causing a whole a barrel of beer to spray out into the cellar. Not a major disaster, but not great for the landlord of the pub. Peter assured him that they would clean up the mess – which he and Mike did together – and would arrange for a replacement barrel free of charge.

There is, however, one task that Peter keeps for himself: tasting the beer. Or at least at first. He takes a few sips and swills them around his mouth, his poker-faced expression giving nothing away. Then it is Mike's turn. For him, this is often the tensest and most exciting moment of the day. Has he done a good job? Does the beer taste the way it should? After taking a mouthful, Mike gives his opinion, which he confines to either 'good' or 'not good'. Usually, he thinks that the result is good, but what will Peter think? In general, Peter agrees, but he tends to explain his reasons in terms of how the installation has positively affected the flavour of the beer, which is something that Mike still finds hard to understand. But that will come with time, Peter assures him. Not that Mike is worried: after all, he still has the rest of his career to refine his beer palate!

Purpose

Work gives you meaning and purpose, and life is *empty* without it. Stephen Hawking

I describe purpose as 'the experience that you mean something, that you can make a difference in the world'. Our search for happiness in recent decades — in fact, in recent centuries — has taught us that it is a utopian dream to expect to be happy at all times and in all places. This is well described in the book *The Happiness Trap* by Russ Harris. Amongst others, researcher Dan Ariely has discovered that purpose is a more powerful motivational driver than happiness or pleasure. Of course, this does not mean that happiness is not important in our lives. It is, but it is not a universal panacea.

In view of the amount of time we spend on it, it is to be hoped that work is one of the things able to bring meaning and purpose into our life. Making a difference, also in an organisational context, is often associated with a desire to contribute towards making the world a better place. This, for many people, is a way to get more satisfaction out of life. And research suggests that people who get more satisfaction out of life are also more resilient and better motivated.

Purpose is an important factor in creating Positive Connections between people in organisations. Working together with your organisation and your colleagues to achieve the same meaningful goal, a goal that can make a real difference to the world, creates unity and a sense of connectedness. We are much better able to put our personal differences to one side if we know that we are pursuing the same mission and trying to realise the same objectives. If I know that you are as dedicated to the mission of the organisation, the department or the team as I am, then I will be much more inclined to follow you and give you my support.

As far as purpose in a working relationship is concerned, for me the most important components are as follows:

The why

If you make money, you might not make *meaning*. Guy Kawasaki

When we talk about meaning and purpose, the most important word is 'why'. Why do we do what we do? What difference do we want to make? How will this contribute to a better world? Who will benefit? Unfortunately, the 'why' question is still not being asked in many organisations. These organisations are too busy explaining what they want to achieve and how they will achieve it, but they often forget to say why they want to achieve it. What is the purpose behind all their initiatives and activities? If they mention reasons at all, they often relate to matters like boosting profits, reducing costs, increasing efficiency, improving quality, etc. They seldom talk about the benefits they want to create for their internal or external customers, or how they hope to meet the needs of various stakeholders, or how they want to have a positive impact on the world...

Ten questions for reflection on the 'why'

- Is the 'why' of your organisation clearly defined in a mission statement or elsewhere?
- Are you aware of the difference that your organisation wants to make/is making in the world?
- Do you know how the products or services of your organisation make a difference in the lives of your customers?
- Do you know your own personal 'why', both privately and professionally?
- Do you know the difference you want to make in the world through your work in your organisation?
- Do you see a connection between your 'why' and the 'why' of your organisation?
- Do you know how your organisation wishes to make a difference in the world? What are its values?
- Do you see a connection between your values and the values of the organisation?
- Do you work and act in accordance with these values? Do you express these values openly?
- Do you stimulate others to work and act in accordance with these values?

Pitfall

The main pitfall associated with too much 'why' is that your goals and your approach may become exaggeratedly principled and idealistic. As a result, you end up refusing to do anything that does not have a clear why and/or does not generate personal meaning. However, it is very unlikely that every activity that has meaning for the organisation will also have meaning for you personally. For example, keeping a close check on costs is meaningful for your organisation, because it allows it to comply with legal and financial regulations, whereas you might regard this as a pointless activity that takes up valuable time that you could be spending on more important things. In other words, there are some support activities in organisations that cannot be avoided, meaningful or not. You can certainly question their purpose, in the hope of eliminating unnecessary bureaucracy, but to refuse to perform them as a matter of principle will only cost you energy (if not your job). Instead, use this energy to do the things that really count, the ultimate 'why' of your organisation.

Translating the why

> ## Words mean more than what is set down on paper. It takes the *human voice* to infuse them with deeper meaning. Maya Angelou

If a 'why' is defined in an organisation, it is often at the highest level of meaning: why does the organisation exist? What is its raison d'être? But in large organisations it often remains unclear to the individual employees exactly how their work contributes towards this big picture. Discussing with your colleagues how this 'why' can be translated to apply to your own department, your own team or even your own individual work is an activity that can give a huge boost to your motivation and engagement. Examine who benefits or becomes better as a result of your work, bearing in mind that this can mean both external and internal customers. In this way, you will discover how you make a difference in your organisation.

Ten questions for reflecting on translating the why
- Do you start every activity with a 'why' question?
- Do you assess for which person each of your activities can make a difference?
- Do you reflect on how your function can make a contribution to the 'why' of the organisation?
- Do you adjust your approach to your work to reflect the 'why' of the organisation?
- Do you explain to others how their work contributes towards the 'why' of the organisation?
- Do you explain to others how their work contributes towards your work, ambitions and satisfaction?
- Do you, together with others, determine your objectives in relation to the 'why' of your organisation, department and team?

- Do you measure, formally or informally, how your work contributes to the 'why' of the organisation?
- Do you listen to your internal/external customers to understand how you make a difference in their lives?
- Do you adjust your objectives and approach on the basis of feedback that you receive from your internal/external customers?

Pitfall

Just as the organisation needs to carry out a number of support activities in order to achieve its real mission, so you too in your own job will be confronted with the need to perform similar support activities. It is a good idea to start every task with a 'why' question, but from time to time you will discover that the answer is 'because it must'. Sometimes you can have an influence on that 'must' but sometimes you cannot. Your attitude should reflect the well-known words of Reinhold Niebuhr: 'Grant me the serenity to accept the things I cannot change, the courage to change the things I can and the wisdom to know the difference'. Do not worry unduly about the things that do not have a clear 'why' or the things that you cannot influence. If you are too concerned with translating the 'why', there will be no room in your approach for pragmatism, which is an essential quality if organisations want to be successful in the world of today.

I follow my hostess, wearing the safety helmet and glasses she has just given me. Alice is the person in charge of this factory, which makes flavourings for the food industry. These flavourings are used in various drinks, cakes, sweets and sauces. Her company is particularly proud that they only work with natural ingredients. Most of their competitors work with artificial chemical substances. The production is strictly regulated, precisely because they wish to retain all the natural goodness of their ingredients. There are strict guidelines for every process, procedure and action, which must be followed to the letter.

Unfortunately, during recent months a few things have started to go wrong, says Alice. The quality control tests carried out by the laboratory have resulted in an increasing number of end products being rejected, because they do not meet the required norms. The reasons for this have nearly always been traced back to human error. In other words, the guidelines for the various processes, procedures and actions are not being properly followed. The employees have already been spoken to about this on a number of occasions, but so far there has been no significant improvement. The problem persists. As a result, I have been called in to see if I can persuade the employees to recognise the importance of working with greater attention and care. I explain to Alice that I am not a specialist in quality training, but in personal leadership. Would she be willing to let me approach the challenge from this different perspective? An approach that would seek to bring out the best in every employee, which in turn would automatically imply a need to pay the best possible attention to the quality norms. Alice thinks for a moment and then nods her approval.

One of the pleasant aspects of my job as a trainer/coach is that I am almost always given the opportunity to talk with my future trainees/coachees, so that we can determine the approach that I will take. In this way, you learn a lot about many different professions, including what motivates people to do their work. When I speak with Alice's production workers, I am struck by how often they refer to 'white powder' and 'green tins'. When I probe further they explain that, irrespective of the actual flavour involved, the flavourings are always a white powder that is packed in identical green tins, before being transferred to a second factory for finishing. The end products can either be a fluid syrup, a mixable paste or a self-melting tablet. They add that some days the production process can be more complex, so that relatively few green tins are produced, whereas on other days the number of tins increases. They do not know the reasons for this, just as (in most cases) they have no idea what particular flavouring is being made on any given day or the purpose for which it will eventually be used. For them, it is all just white powder and green tins.

Instead of organising a training course, I agree with Alice that the 'green tins' should be given a photo label that shows the final form of the flavourings, as they will be used by the customer. The label will also contain details of the name of the end product and how much of it can be produced with the contents of the tin. We further agree that a number of videos (already available in the marketing department) will be played in the work cafeteria, in which satisfied customers explain the difference that the company's flavourings have made to the quality of the *products that they in turn make for their own customers. In this way, the production workers will realise that they are not working with white powder in green tins, but with nameable products that allow hundreds of thousands of people to enjoy their favourite meals each day, thanks to the company's healthy and natural flavourings.*

Oh yes, I almost forgot: production quality returned to the desired level within a matter of weeks. The production workers now understand the impact that their contribution can have on the organisation's mission and the importance to this contribution of strictly following the quality guidelines, processes and procedures.

Actions speak louder than words

> The **world** is changed by
> your ***example***, not
> by your ***opinion***. Paulo Coelho

Even if you say all the right things, you will not create Positive Connections unless you translate your words into actions. Positive Connections are being built each day, connections that focus on the other. People who only think about themselves or, even worse, display egotistic behaviour will find it very hard, if not impossible, to make Positive Connections. The more you actively invest in these Positive Connections, the greater the likelihood that other people will invest in Positive Connections with you. The more personal leadership you show, the more you will encourage others to accept their own personal leadership.

Ten questions for reflecting on why actions speak louder than words

- Is your behaviour in keeping with your words and intentions?
- Do you give attention to others?
- Do you make time for others?
- Do you talk and act in a tactful way?
- Do you respect everyone's dignity?
- Do you treat others as they want to be treated?
- Are you approachable?
- Do you invest time and attention in small acts of kindness and gratitude?
- Are you authentic in word and deed?
- Are you 100% present in the moment?

Conclusion

It is up to you to decide which components of Positive Connection you will use more or less frequently. In most cases, you will probably discover that the nature of the (work) relationship will influence this decision. For example, you might find it easier to exchange opinions with your colleagues than with your boss. Or you might take more account of the needs of your customers than those of your team members. There is no unique and universal recipe that will result in the finished dish tasting exactly the same for everyone. In short, you will develop a personal form of Positive Connection, depending on your own preferences and the preference of those to whom you wish to relate. In this respect, authenticity and sincerity are the key words. If necessary, you can modify your style and behaviour to take account of others, but you must always, without exception, remain true to who you are. This brings us to the following section of the book: Authentic Adaptability.

GUIDING PRINCIPLE 2
AUTHENTIC ADAPTABILITY

> Until you make the **unconscious** conscious, it will direct *your life* and you will call it *fate*. _{Carl Jung}

Authenticity

The second guiding principle, Authentic Adaptability, makes a powerful contribution towards Positive Connection. According to the Oxford English Dictionary, authentic means 'worthy of acceptance or belief, the quality of being genuine or true'. You can also translate this as 'being yourself'. What you say and do is real, and not fake. On the basis of this definition, the link with the guiding principle of Positive Connection is clear. Unless we are in a theatre or watching a film, 'play acting' does not generate connection. The feeling that someone is playing a role quickly leads to distrust or to the suspicion that we are being manipulated. If the colleague who normally walks past your desk each morning without saying a word suddenly pulls up a chair, offers to get you a coffee and asks enthusiastically how you are, you will probably feel just a little bit sceptical about his intentions. Fake behaviour does not inspire the kind of leadership that will make you want to follow others.

Multiple versions of yourself

We often talk about authenticity and authentic leadership as though there is just one version of yourself. A single version that talks and acts the same way every day, irrespective of the context and the situation. If you can discover this unique version of yourself, you will have self-insight and insight into your style of leadership. In reality, however, things are more complex. We show different versions of ourselves in different situations. If you intervene in a furious discussion between two of your colleagues, you might do so cautiously, carefully and with great empathy, while just an hour later you speak with great passion and fire to a client about your proposal. Does this mean that in one of these two situations you are not being authentic? No, it simply means that you are showing two different sides of yourself. Context and situation have a clear influence on our behaviour.

When it comes to determining behaviour, is context a more powerful influencer than personality, or is it the other way around? In recent decades, the pendulum has swung in both directions in academic and professional debate. And it is indeed a matter on which a definitive conclusion is unlikely to be reached. All we can say with any certainty is that both factors – context and personality – have an impact on our behaviour and approach.

Self-monitoring

Psychologist Mark Snyder discovered that some people do have a tendency to react the same way, irrespective of context, whereas others are more inclined to adjust their reaction to reflect the situation, while still remaining authentic. He described this latter group of people as having the ability to self-monitor themselves. In contrast, this first group displays a lower level of self-monitoring. You can compare people who have a high level of self-monitoring with a chameleon: they change colour to match the environment in which they find themselves, but they remain a chameleon.

This (not unreasonably) raises the question of whether or not someone who frequently changes his behaviour to reflect the context can still be regarded as authentic. The answer to this question is an unequivocal 'yes'. We can refer to this as style flexibility or Authentic Adaptability. For example, we probably all know people at work who are mild-mannered in their general office behaviour, but who are transformed instantly into, say, a tough negotiator if a supplier asks for an over-inflated price. We can experience this person as being authentic in both situations. However, this is only the case if the intention behind the change of behaviour to reflect the context is genuine and positive. Positive intention – the wish to do something good – is therefore a necessary condition.

Self-insight

> **When you are living the best version of** yourself, **you** *inspire* **others to live the best** versions **of** *themselves.* Steve Maraboli

Do you remember our definition of leadership as 'a process of self-insight and positive influencing with the aim of bringing out the best in yourself and in others, in order to achieve the objectives of the organisation'? Before we make any attempt to 'bring out the best in others', it is important that we have sufficient self-insight or self-awareness. That is what we will explore in this chapter. What does 'bringing out the best in yourself' actually mean? Amongst other things, it means having insight into what the best possible version(s) of yourself look(s) like and the different ways in which you can be authentic. Last but not least, this chapter will also show us just how great our capacity to adapt truly is, how easy it is to self-monitor, and what different styles of leadership we can easily adopt.

Self-insight consists of three important components:
- Knowing what you know and are able to do. And knowing what you do not know and are not able to do.
- Knowing who you are. And knowing who you are not.
- Knowing what you want. And knowing what you do not want.

How you answer these questions forms the basis for your personal leadership, which in turn forms the basis for all other forms of leadership. Three seemingly simple questions, but finding the right answers often involves a challenging search for the truth.

Knowing what you know and are able to do is perhaps the least difficult of the three questions. Knowing who you are and, above all, what you want is often much harder and demands some serious self-investigation. Moreover, the answers to these questions also change and evolve over time. For many of us, this process is a never-ending story, which repeatedly throws up new insights and new answers. In the following section, I will discuss a number of techniques that can help you to acquire the necessary self-insight. You might already have done 'exercises' of this kind in the past. If so, feel free to include those results. The more input you have, the more accurate and more nuanced your self-insight will be. At the same time, make sure that you do not set the bar too high. None of us is capable of mapping out our entire personality. Focus instead on the most important strong points on which you wish to build and also on the most important weaker points that you would like to change or improve. If you devote sufficient attention to these matters, you can refine your self-insight little by little each day. Like life as a whole, self-insight is a journey, not a destination.

Knowing what you know and are able to do

Mastering others is strength. Mastering yourself is *true power.* Lao-Tze

As already mentioned, the first question is possibly the least difficult to answer, especially if we are talking about 'hard' competencies, such as technical knowledge and skills. We all know what we studied in the past and what expertise we have built up over the years.

However, the so-called 'soft' competencies, such as interpersonal skills, are often much trickier to assess. We all have our 'blind spots', skills that we think we possess (or do not possess), but where the perception of others is different. As a result, we all have unknown or underestimated strengths and weaknesses. In this respect, feedback from others can work wonders if we want to get accurate and true insight into what we know and are able to do, and what not.

Figure 1 is a generic list with thirty competencies that can be useful in organisations. For each of these competences, note down your own assessment of the extent to which you possess the competence, using the following procedure:
- I can do this well:
  - 10 = I can do this so well that I can coach others in it.
  - … => …
  - 5 = I can do this sufficiently well to carry out my work effectively, but no more.
  - … => …
- 0 = I cannot do this at all.

- I like doing this (I would like to do this):
  - 10 = I really like doing this; it gives me great energy.
  - … => …
  - 5 = It costs me no energy to do this, but it gives me no energy, either.
  - … => …
  - 0 = I do not like doing this at all; it eats up all my energy.

If you think that there are competencies missing from this list that are relevant for your organisation and/or work, please feel free to add them. In the column 'I like doing this', you can also indicate competencies that you have not yet mastered, but would like to possess. These could become important learning opportunities.

If you want to develop an even more accurate picture of yourself, it is a good idea to give the list to others and ask them to fill in what they think about your competencies, giving you a score for each one, supplemented with frank, open comments about your strong and less strong points. These comments from others often contain the most useful information of all!

	Competence	I can do this well	I like doing this	Feedback Colleague 1	Feedback Colleague 2	Feedback Colleague ...
1	Managing					
2	Advising					
3	Analysing					
4	Influencing					
5	Deciding					
6	Coaching					
7	Communicating					
8	Solving conflicts					
9	Delegating					
10	Persevering					
11	Informing					
12	Initiating					
13	Empathising					
14	Innovating					
15	Inspiring					
16	Sharing knowledge					
17	Listening					
18	Motivating					
19	Networking					
20	Negotiating					
21	Undertaking					
22	Showing enterprise					
23	Persuading					
24	Planning					
25	Setting priorities					
26	Solving problems					
27	Collaborating					
28	Developing strategies					
29	Implementing					
30	Improving					
31	...					
32	...					
33	...					
34	...					
35	...					

▶ Figure 1. **List of competencies that can be relevant in organisations**

On the basis of Figure 1, taking account of your own comments and those of others, draw up a list of your top ten competencies that give (or would give) you the most pleasure to possess/perform. Describe each of these competencies in your own words. Do not underestimate the importance of this exercise. What does each competence mean for you? How would you give them personal shape and form? Where and when would you use them?

Here are some examples of possible personal descriptions of a competence:
- **Persevering**: 'If problems arise during a project with my team, I am often the one who comes up with an original solution, long after the others have stopped trying. '
- **Listening**: 'In our team meetings I listen to everyone's opinions and am good at summarising them concisely.'
- **Persuading**: 'If new safety measures are introduced in the production section, they often meet with initial resistance. In dialogue, I am usually able to persuade the production staff to comply with the new measures.'
- **Implementing**: 'I carry out lab tests efficiently and with precision, including completion of the necessary reports.'

In terms of 'bringing out the best in yourself', this list provides you with a useful summary of competencies that will allow you to make a difference in your organisation. By answering the following questions, you will be able to see how you can harness and deploy your talents even more meaningfully:

- Which competencies can I use in which situations?
- Who in my personal working environment and in the wider organisation can benefit from my competencies?
- Which of my tasks are most suited to making use of my competencies?
- How can I help to realise the objectives of my team/department/organisation by using my competencies?
- Which competencies do I still not use enough?
- Which competencies do I use too much?
- Which competencies (that I like to use) can I or do I want to develop further?
  How and where can these competencies be developed?
  Who can help me?

Knowing who you are

> The best leaders don't know just one style of *leadership*, they're skilled at several and have the *flexibility* to switch between styles as the circumstances dictate. Daniel Goleman

Who are you? Who are you not? When searching for the answers to these questions, personality models can certainly play a useful role. At the same time, also remember to take into account the important comment by the famous statistician George Box, who once said: 'All models are wrong, but some are useful.' There are currently 7 billion people living on our planet and each of them is unique. You, me, everyone. It is impossible to describe all of us with 100 % accuracy with just a single model. Even so, a model can give us useful indicators and a frame of reference to better understand ourselves.

To help you discover your natural and preferred leadership styles, for The Leadership Connection I have developed a model based on the psychology of Carl Jung. But before describing it, I repeat George Box's words of warning: it may not be the most accurate model, but it is one that can reveal some useful insights and is also widely used. In this respect, Jung's psychology forms the basis for several well-known personality models, such as MBTI™, Insights Discovery™, DISC™ and Social Styles™. This means that if you search for and find your natural behavioural styles in your work environment by using one of these models, you will also automatically find your natural and preferred leadership styles in The Leadership Connection. Likewise, if you discover your preferred behavioural styles through a different model, such as Big Five™ or Hexaco™, this also forms a good basis for further determining your preferred styles of leadership.

Carl Jung makes a distinction between different personality preferences by combining three separate dimensions:
- Introvert ◄► Extrovert
- Sensing ◄► Intuitive
- Thinking ◄► Feeling

In Figure 2, I list a series of opposing qualities for each of these dimensions.

Introvert	Extrovert
Behind the scenes	In public
Listening	Speaking
Thinking, then speaking	Thinking while speaking
One-to-one conversation	Group interaction
Single-tasking	Multi-tasking
Reserved	Flamboyant
Plan-oriented	Action-oriented
Thoughtful	Outspoken
Careful	Daring
Consider, then decide	Decide quickly

Sensing	iNtuitive
Traditional	Innovative
Factual	Abstract
Realistic	Inventive
Focused on the present	Focused on the future
Operational	Visionary
Detail-oriented	Broad view
Procedures and rules	Improvisation
Practical	Ideas
Routine	Variation
Steady tempo	Fluctuating tempo

Thinking	Feeling
Formal	Personal
Analytical	Considerate
Detached	Engaged
Convincing	Receptive
Competitive	Amenable
Discussion	Harmony
Direct	Tactful
Objective	Subjective
Task-oriented	Relation-oriented
Processes and systems	Culture

▶ Figure 2. **Opposing characteristics for the three dimensions of C.G. Jung**

These three dimensions, each with two opposing possibilities, result in a total of eight behavioural styles. In The Leadership Connection I have translated these styles into eight leadership styles or preferences. It is up to you to decide which preference to use in which context, and also to decide which styles come more naturally to you (and will therefore be used more often) and which ones are less easy for you to adopt (and will therefore be used less often). By combining these two decisions, you will be able to see which styles you will be likely to use more or less often in different contexts. However, it is important to remember that there is no such thing as a 'good' style or a 'bad' style. All you can say is that some styles are better suited to certain contexts than others.

On the following pages you will find a summary of each of the eight leadership styles, as I use them in The Leadership Connection. For each leadership style you will find the following information:

- the associated talents and preferences;
- the most important characteristics;
- the strengths;
- an example of these strengths in practice;
- the possible pitfalls;
- an example of these pitfalls in practice;
- possible points for development.

Remember that the pitfalls often occur because of an exaggerated emphasis on a particular preference or talent. For example, 'too assertive' can sometimes cross over into 'aggressive'; 'too factual' can be seen as 'cold and impersonal'; 'too optimistic' can be regarded as 'naive'. The nature of the environment can also play a role in determining whether or not a pitfall arises. For example, in a rational, technical environment you are less likely to be branded as 'cold and impersonal' than in a highly social, assistance-providing environment.

For each leadership style, one of the potential pitfalls will be marked with a letter C, standing for 'control drama'. This is based on the theory of the philosopher and psychologist James Redfield, as illustrated in his book *The Celestine Prophecy*. He makes a distinction between four types of control dramas that people use to attract attention to themselves, so that they can gain control over the situation in which they find themselves. The four control dramas are:

- Intimidation   controlling the situation through intimidatory behaviour;
- Interrogation   controlling the situation through endless critical questioning;
- Aloofness   controlling the situation by withdrawing from it to demand attention;
- 'Poor me'   controlling the situation by seeking sympathy and making others feel guilty.

There are various ways in which you can discover your personal leadership style preferences using The Leadership Connection classification system, as described above:

- You indicate your preferences between the opposing characteristics of the three dimensions detailed in Figure 2 and then search for your preferred leadership styles on this basis. For example, if you think that you are predominantly 'Introvert' and 'Sensing' (as opposed to 'Extrovert' and 'Intuitive'), but are roughly 50/50 when it comes to 'Thinking' and 'Feeling', your preferred leadership styles are likely to be IST (Introvert, Sensing, Thinking) and ISF (Introvert, Sensing, Feeling).
- You read the descriptions and examples for each of the eight leadership styles and mark/note down the words — which will often be adjectives — that most appeal to you in terms of how you see your leadership. The leadership styles for which you have marked or noted down the most words will most probably be your natural leadership styles.
- You read the descriptions of each of the eight leadership styles and give a score to each style, depending on the extent to which you can recognise yourself in that style.
- You can also ask your colleagues to complete this exercise on your behalf, making use of one of the three above mentioned methods. In this way, you will immediately get a good idea of how you are perceived within the organisation.
- Last but not least, you can use all four of the above methods and compare the results they yield.

As in so many other things, the method you choose will be dependent on your preferences.

Directive leadership – EST

Extrovert	Sensing	Thinking
In public	Traditional	Formal
Speaking	Factual	Analytical
Thinking while speaking	Realistic	Detached
Group interaction	Focused on the present	Convincing
Multi-tasking	Operational	Competitive
Flamboyant	Detail-oriented	Discussion
Action-oriented	Procedures and rules	Direct
Outspoken	Practical	Objective
Daring	Routine	Task-oriented
Decide quickly	Steady tempo	Processes and systems

▶ Figure 3. **The directive leader**

Characteristics:
- Driven
- Efficient
- Pragmatic
- Decisive
- Delegation and control
- Problem solver

The strengths of the directive leader

Directive leaders are pragmatic and efficient. They like to see results quickly. When making decisions, they allow themselves to be led by a rational analysis of the facts. They prefer to focus on operational tasks and are expert at finding practical solutions. Their approach to their work is factual and realistic. They are happy to delegate but check to see that the delegated tasks are being carried out in the manner they had previously agreed. They are driven and competitive. They dare to take risks, but only calculated ones. They organise work on the basis of clear processes and guidelines.

> *Carla works in an advertising bureau, where she develops campaigns for a single major customer in the world of telecommunications. She does not have her own permanent team, but puts together a temporary team of insiders and outsiders for each new campaign, depending on its nature. She has made her own procedural manual for the creation of advertising campaigns, a manual that she follows to the letter. She also uses this manual to devise a plan and to allocate roles and responsibilities to others. In this way, she can monitor and control everything in an orderly manner. The people who work for her regularly know that she expects the campaign to make progress rapidly. However, this haste means that she is often confronted with unexpected problems and challenges. While others might be tempted to throw in the towel in this situation, Carla always finds a solution. As soon as she is sure that the people she is working with are on the right track, she moves on to her next activity. However, she phones all her people regularly to check on how things are going. If there are questions or decisions that need to be made, she deals with them instantly. In her office she has a standing table that she uses for meetings, so that she can be sure that the discussions will be short and to the point. She hates unnecessary waste of time.*

The directive leader – possible pitfalls:

- Status-conscious
- Ruthless
- Intimidating (C)
- Unfeeling
- Impatient
- Conservative

Directive leaders sometimes want to move forward at such a pace that others find it hard to keep up with them. As a result, these others can quickly become exhausted, not only because of the speed but also because the leader pays too little attention to their needs and requirements. These leaders do not like to deviate from their chosen course, which means that they are not always receptive to the creative ideas of their people. If things are not going the way they hoped, they frequently have a tendency to delve into the details of the situation, so that there is a risk that they will begin to micro-manage. Sometimes they are so occupied with this 'hands-on' approach that they fail to take the necessary time to step back and refocus on a clear vision for the future. If they are under pressure, they might resort to intimidation, if this is the only way to concentrate attention and power in their own hands.

> For Carla, the most difficult aspect of her job is working with the creative people in her office. They sometimes come up with the wildest schemes that disrupt her planning and turn the whole project upside down. She often thinks that these people don't know the meaning of the word 'deadline'! This can lead to heated discussions, during which she needs to use all her reserves of patience to remain calm. When the advertising spots have been created, she usually sits next to the film editor to help with the selection of the images. What's more, she dares to interfere with even the smallest details. Occasionally, she hires in actors for these films, but there are already several who no longer wish to work with her. They think she pays too little attention to their artistic opinions, so that in consequence they feel misunderstood. In their eyes, her constant pushing damages the quality of the end result.

Everyone Can Lead

Introvert	iNtuitive	Feeling
Behind the scenes	Innovative	Personal
Listening	Abstract	Considerate
Thinking, then speaking	Inventive	Engaged
One-to-one conversation	Focused on the future	Receptive
Single-tasking	Visionary	Amenable
Reserved	Broad view	Harmony
Plan-oriented	Improvisation	Tactful
Thoughtful	Ideas	Subjective
Careful	Variation	Relation-oriented
Consider, then decide	Fluctuating tempo	Culture

▶ Figure 4. **Possible points for development for a directive leader**

Entrepreneurial leadership – ENT

Extrovert	iNtuitive	Thinking
In public	Innovative	Formal
Speaking	Abstract	Analytical
Thinking while speaking	Inventive	Detached
Group interaction	Focused on the future	Convincing
Multi-tasking	Visionary	Competitive
Flamboyant	Broad view	Discussion
Action-oriented	Improvisation	Direct
Outspoken	Ideas	Objective
Daring	Variation	Task-oriented
Decide quickly	Fluctuating tempo	Processes and systems

▶ Figure 5. **The entrepreneurial leader**

Characteristics:

- Assertive
- Straightforward
- Ambitious
- Target-oriented
- Bold
- Competitive

The strengths of the entrepreneurial leader

Entrepreneurial leaders are assertive, focused and target-oriented. They are also competitive and like to see quick results. When making decisions, they do what seems logical and practical. They concentrate heavily on achieving the ambitious mission that they have set for themselves and others. To make this possible, their approach to their work is inventive and innovative. What's more, they are able to motivate those around them by their personal example and their inspirational vision. They are prepared to be opportunistic and will not shrink from taking risks, even if it is not possible to analyse all the possible consequences beforehand. Any problems that they meet will be solved along the way, preferably without stopping.

> Kevin is an IT expert and works as an independent analyst-programmer for major companies. Initially, he worked for a large software company, but he found that things were moving too slowly for his liking. He was so irritated by too much office politics, too many rules and too much bureaucracy that one day he took the impulsive decision to set up in business on his own. Things went well and in the meantime he has developed a network of other freelance IT specialists, so that they can position themselves better in the market and ask for more competitive prices for their services. Kevin seems to be good at attracting new customers. As a result, he not only earns good money for his own technical work, but also for the projects he sub-contracts to his other IT contacts, with whom he has made clear agreements about prices and margins. He dreams of expanding this network still further and hopes to one day go international with the concept. A Dutch customer recently asked if he could do some work for him in The Netherlands and Kevin accepted almost without thinking, even though he currently has no IT partners in that country.

The entrepreneurial leader – possible pitfalls

- Nonchalant
- Ruthless
- Intimidating (C)
- Unfeeling
- Impatient
- Easily bored

Entrepreneurial leaders are so competitive that they do not always stick to the rules in their ruthless pursuit of their objectives. To achieve their goals, they are willing to make personal sacrifices and expect others to do the same. As a result, they also expect huge flexibility from their people, but take little account of what this might mean for those concerned. Once they have started a new project, they very quickly move on to the next one. Solving problems and tying up the practical loose ends of previous ventures is something they tend to leave to others. If they do need to get involved in problem-solving, their solutions are usually curative. Taking time in advance to develop preventative solutions is not their strong point. Sometimes they are juggling so many balls in the air that others find it hard to see where they should begin to tackle the multiplicity of tasks with which they are faced.

For Kevin, the most difficult aspect of his job is to facilitate the (informal) networking among the freelancers he works with. Too many of these freelancers want to get to know their other 'colleagues' better and also want to have a listening ear in the network to whom they can turn for advice when they run into problems. These are not immediate priorities for Kevin, who regards dealing with such personal concerns as an energy-consuming waste of time. If he wants to launch a new idea within the network, he often gets the feeling that he has to really push the others hard before they are willing to fall in line behind him. They keep on asking tiresome practical questions for which Kevin does not yet have an answer. He sometimes thinks that they are deliberately working against him! Kevin recently won his first contract in The Netherlands. It is a good project with work for four IT technicians. However, he has so far been unable to get the project off the ground, because no one in the current Belgian network is prepared to go and work across the border. As a result, Kevin is now frantically searching for Dutch IT freelancers who can act on his behalf.

Introvert	Sensing	Feeling
Behind the scenes	Traditional	Personal
Listening	Factual	Considerate
Thinking then speaking	Realistic	Engaged
One-to-one conversation	Focused on the present	Receptive
Single-tasking	Operational	Amenable
Reserved	Detail-oriented	Harmony
Plan-oriented	Procedures and rules	Tactful
Thoughtful	Practical	Subjective
Careful	Routine	Relation-oriented
Consider, then decide	Steady tempo	Culture

▶ Figure 6. **Possible points for development for an entrepreneurial leader**

Inspirational leadership – ENF

Extrovert	iNtuition	Feeling
In public	Innovative	Personal
Speaking	Abstract	Considerate
Thinking while speaking	Inventive	Engaged
Group interaction	Focused on the future	Receptive
Multi-tasking	Visionary	Amenable
Flamboyant	Broad view	Harmony
Action-oriented	Improvisation	Tactful
Outspoken	Ideas	Subjective
Daring	Variation	Relation-oriented
Decide quickly	Fluctuating tempo	Culture

▶ Figure 7. **The inspirational leader**

Characteristics:

- Innovative
- Enthusing
- Mobilising
- Charismatic
- Motivating
- Dynamic

The strengths of the inspirational leader

Inspirational leaders can enthuse and motivate others. They love innovation, new ideas and brainstorming. When making decisions, they allow themselves to be led by the things they find interesting and exciting. However, they first weigh up all the possible opportunities, but then balance this against the possible impact of the opportunities on those around them. They like to focus on the realisation of a creative vision. They are able to inspire others for the same purpose by sharing with them all the possibilities that the vision potentially has to offer. They always try to involve these others in what they are doing and are receptive to creative ideas. Their enthusiasm is infectious and they are always willing to give people the opportunity to carry out their appointed tasks in an autonomous manner.

Emmy is an exercise expert with a passion for technology. She is a reasonably good amateur athlete and knows everything there is to know about the latest sports watches, racing bikes and running shoes. In the hospital where she works she is always the first person to test out new equipment and devices, following which she then explains all their possibilities with great enthusiasm to her colleagues. Some of her older colleagues are not keen on these modern innovations, but Emmy is always able to convince them to give the new technology a chance. Each year she also manages to persuade some of her other colleagues to accompany her to the annual trade fair for fitness equipment. For her, this is the equivalent of being a kid in a candy store, although in her case the 'candy' consists of energy drinks and sports foods. Back at the hospital, she not only enthuses the other exercise experts in her own department, but also visits the paramedics in other departments to involve them in her story. They sometimes have to smile at her 'whirlwind' approach, but the pleasure with which she communicates her message means that everyone is happy to listen.

The inspirational leader – possible pitfalls
- 'Weather vane' (turns with the wind)
- Nonchalant
- 'Poor me' (C)
- Over-sensitive
- Impatient
- Easily bored

Inspirational leaders often have so many ideas that they are seldom able to realise them all. Their computer screen is covered in post-it notes, whose number seems to increase all the time. This means that others often wait to see which way the wind is blowing before committing themselves. Will anything come of it or is this just another wild scheme that will lead nowhere? Inspirational leaders can sometimes take criticism of their ideas personally, but to avoid conflict they are reluctant to discuss such criticism. They also often have difficulty seeing the practical implications of their ideas and are not very good when it comes to detail and planning. Remaining focused on a project until all the loose ends are tied up is another challenge they frequently fail to meet.

> For Emmy, the most difficult aspect of her job is the routine tasks she has to perform. She recently introduced a new type of home trainer into her department, which needs to be reset and maintained each week. Emmy's colleagues regularly need to remind her on Monday morning that the home trainer is not ready for use (again). Emmy then tries to put everything in order in a frantic rush, but instead of following the manual she prefers to do things 'her own way', which actually takes much longer. A few months ago, another new piece of equipment was installed; namely, a rowing machine. Ever since it arrived, the machine has been showing an 'error' message in one of its programmes. Her colleagues have already asked her half a dozen times to contact the supplier, but so far she has failed to do so. She is disappointed in herself that she has let her colleagues down and tries to keep out of their way to avoid difficult conversations and their possible criticism.

Everyone Can Lead

Introvert	Sensing	Thinking
Behind the scenes	Traditional	Formal
Listening	Factual	Analytical
Thinking then speaking	Realistic	Detached
One-to-one conversation	Focused on the present	Convincing
Single-tasking	Operational	Competitive
Reserved	Detail-oriented	Discussion
Plan-oriented	Procedures and rules	Direct
Thoughtful	Practical	Objective
Careful	Routine	Task-oriented
Consider, then decide	Steady tempo	Processes and systems

▶Figure 8. **Possible points for development for an inspirational leader**

Connective leadership – ESF

Extrovert	Sensing	Feeling
In public	Traditional	Personal
Speaking	Factual	Considerate
Thinking while speaking	Realistic	Engaged
Group interaction	Focused on the present	Receptive
Multi-tasking	Operational	Amenable
Flamboyant	Detail-oriented	Harmony
Action-oriented	Procedures and rules	Tactful
Outspoken	Practical	Subjective
Daring	Routine	Relation-oriented
Decide quickly	Steady tempo	Culture

▶Figure 9. **The connective leader**

Characteristics
- Networker
- Team builder
- Encouraging
- Ambassador
- Flexible
- Generous

The strengths of the connective leader

Connective leaders build on their relationships and networks with the aim of moving people in a particular direction. They like to find creative and consensual solutions through brainstorming with all the relevant stakeholders. When making decisions, they take into consideration the interests and feelings of everyone concerned. At the same time, they are also aware that the solution needs to be realistic and feasible. Their approach to their work is problem-solving and their optimism contributes towards an atmosphere of positive collaboration with others. They attach great importance to respecting not only their own values, but also the values of those with whom they interact. They regard every problem as an opportunity.

René works for the government agency that is responsible for nature conservation. He is passionate about protecting the environment and does his job with heart and soul. Nature conservation is a complex matter that involves many different parties, often with opposing interests. For example, local farmers and project developers seldom have much enthusiasm for complying with the conditions set down in worldwide climate agreements. Although he shares his idealism with his colleagues and others with whom he interacts, he is convinced that he can only achieve meaningful results if he can mobilise relevant people and organisations to start moving in the right direction. His main objective is to get everyone sitting around the same table, so that they can search for solutions together. He organises and chairs these meetings with great enthusiasm, leading the discussions in a non-directive manner towards constructive decisions. He knows all his conversation partners through and through, and is expert at manoeuvring his way through the political minefield that so often surrounds nature conservation issues. In this way, he is usually able to secure a measure of agreement.

The connective leader – possible pitfalls
- 'Weather vane' (turns with the wind)
- Status-conscious
- 'Poor me' (C)
- Over-sensitive
- Impatient
- Conservative

Connective leaders sometimes take too much account of the opinions of others, so that their own opinions and interests are pushed into the background. They tend to follow the person they are talking with at any given moment. If two groups disagree about who should perform a particular task, connective leaders often intervene and suggest that they can do it instead. In this way, they hope to avoid conflict. However, this quality, combined with their endless optimism, means that they often underestimate the amount of work they have to do, so that they fail to complete tasks by the agreed deadlines. If things start to get on top of them, they frequently respond in an emotional manner and adopt a 'poor me' role that seeks to attract the attention of those around them. Even so, they continue to take on tasks and problems that are almost impossible to implement and solve, largely because they fail to set reasonable conditions in advance. In their desire to reach a consensus, they often sacrifice important results simply to keep everyone satisfied.

> *René sometimes finds it difficult to take the tough decisions that are necessary to reach a quick solution. He is afraid that if he does this he will anger everyone, leading to conflicts that will be even more difficult to resolve. As a result, it often takes a long time before any concrete results are seen. He was recently able to broker an agreement between a number of environmental organisations and the farmers association. The agreed terms were set down in a sizeable document that was accepted by both sides. It was a good solution for the short term, but it lacked a long-term vision for the future. At the moment, René, at the request of the competent minister, is conducting negotiations with various industry groups in an attempt to reduce the level of air pollution. He is proud that the minister has entrusted him with this task, but he thinks that the objectives he has been set are not realistic. Even so, he accepted the task without comment or conditions. After all,*

he doesn't want to question or come into conflict with an important government minister! René knows that the industrial representatives are expecting him to put forward the government's long-term vision on air pollution, but he finds this difficult. He prefers to solve current practical problems, rather than developing long-term strategies.

Introvert	iNtuition	Thinking
Behind the scenes	Innovative	Formal
Listening	Abstract	Analytical
Thinking then speaking	Inventive	Detached
One-to-one conversation	Focused on the future	Convincing
Single-tasking	Visionary	Competitive
Reserved	Broad view	Discussion
Plan-oriented	Improvisation	Direct
Thoughtful	Ideas	Objective
Careful	Variation	Task-oriented
Consider, then decide	Fluctuating tempo	Processes and systems

▶ Figure 10. **Possible points for development for a connective leader**

Serving leadership – INF

Introvert	iNtuitive	Feeling
Behind the scenes	Innovative	Personal
Listening	Abstract	Considerate
Thinking then speaking	Inventive	Engaged
One-to-one conversation	Focused on the future	Receptive
Single-tasking	Visionary	Amenable
Reserved	Broad view	Harmony
Plan-oriented	Improvisation	Tactful
Thoughtful	Ideas	Subjective
Careful	Variation	Relation-oriented
Consider, then decide	Fluctuating tempo	Culture

▶ Figure 11. **The serving leader**

Characteristics
- Supportive
- Loyal
- Inventive
- Considerate
- Empathic
- Democratic

The strengths of the serving leader

Serving leaders are empathic and caring. They are excellent listeners and know the people with whom they work through and through. They are often driven by a vision that has significant (societal) meaning. Working together with others to realise this vision gives them great energy. When making decisions, they allow themselves to be guided by the vision and by the impact it will have on everyone concerned. Because they are democratically minded, they also like to involve their team in the decision-making process. They know exactly how to encourage people to give the best of themselves. At the same time, they are innovative and considered in their approach. They are always available for those with whom they work and are happy to support them in their efforts to achieve the desired results.

> *Olivia has been working as a production assistant in a biscuit factory for twenty years. She is currently the 'libero' on the production line for chocolate biscuits. 'Libero' means that she has no fixed place on the line but instead has a free role, which allows her to help out wherever necessary, so that the line can continue to function at full capacity. If the packing boxes at the end of the line fail to close properly, she is there to seal them down. If the chocolate supply unit looks like blocking (again), she is on hand to find a creative solution that will keep the chocolate flowing. Thanks to her many years of experience, she is familiar with all the different 'stations' on the production line and knows the problems that are likely to occur. When new employees join the line, it is Olivia who explains what they have to do and helps them to get started. She really enjoys her work and regularly passes down the line, encouraging 'her' people with a pat on the back or a word of friendly advice. If she has time, she will even cross over to other production lines, to see if she can lend a helping hand there. At the end of a shift, Olivia always stays behind for a few extra minutes. This is not part of her job and she is not obliged to do it, but she wants to make sure that the transfer from her shift to the next one runs smoothly, so that there are no negative effects for the production line.*

The serving leader – possible pitfalls
- Wanting to please
- Dreamer
- Aloof (C)
- Over-sensitive
- Doubting
- Easily bored

Serving leaders have a real dislike of conflict and often find it difficult to deal with criticism, which they can sometimes take personally. At the same time, they are reluctant to criticise others, because they are afraid that this will damage 'good relations'. If two people disagree about who should do a particular task, they will often take over the task themselves, so that conflict can be avoided. This can result in them having too many things to do and too many deadlines to meet, which can make them feel uncomfortable, because they have to set priorities and sometimes say 'no', which goes against their nature and their desire to help everyone. They are not good at routine tasks and like to have variety in their work. If they think that their help is not being properly appreciated, they can sometimes behave aloofly, in an effort to attract attention.

> For Olivia, the most difficult aspect of her job is when 'her' production line experiences different problems in different places at the same time. This means that different colleagues need her assistance and she would like to help them all, but she cannot be in two places at once. In these situations, she often takes decisions about where to intervene that are not wholly rational. She allows herself to be influenced by the colleagues who shout the loudest or show the most frustration. However, this can sometimes result in other colleagues telling her that she should first have devoted her attention elsewhere. When this happens, it all gets a bit too much for Olivia: the pressure to get the production line running again, the comments of her colleagues, everybody watching to see what she will do next... Sometimes others offer to help, but she prefers to solve the problems herself, because she feels that this is her responsibility. As soon as the line is operational again, she will often disappear to the rest room for several minutes to recover her composure. She takes the comments that others have made during the 'incident' to heart and feels that she has let everyone down. She is pleased if someone from another production line comes into the rest room, so that she can tell her side of the story.

Extrovert	Sensing	Thinking
In public	Traditional	Formal
Speaking	Factual	Analytical
Thinking while speaking	Realistic	Detached
Group interaction	Focused on the present	Convincing
Multi-tasking	Operational	Competitive
Flamboyant	Detail-oriented	Discussion
Action-oriented	Procedures and rules	Direct
Outspoken	Practical	Objective
Daring	Routine	Task-oriented
Decide quickly	Steady tempo	Processes and systems

▶ Figure 12. **Possible points for development for a serving leader**

Participative leadership – ISF

Introvert	Sensing	Feeling
Behind the scenes	Traditional	Personal
Listening	Factual	Considerate
Thinking then speaking	Realistic	Engaged
One-to-one conversation	Focused on the present	Receptive
Single-tasking	Operational	Amenable
Reserved	Detail-oriented	Harmony
Plan-oriented	Procedures and rules	Tactful
Thoughtful	Practical	Subjective
Careful	Routine	Relation-oriented
Consider, then decide	Steady tempo	Culture

▶ Figure 13. **The participative leader**

- Inclusive
- Thoughtful
- Engaged
- Conscientious
- Adaptive
- Value-driven

The strengths of the participative leader

Participative leaders are dedicated and conscientious. They will ensure that everyone in their team feels at home. Their approach to their work is well considered and they pay the necessary attention to detail. When making decisions, they are led by the facts, their values and the practical implications for all concerned. They are able to adjust easily and can put their own interests to one side for the benefit of the ambitions, preferences and interests of others. They do their work competently, thoroughly and with a minimum of fuss. At the same time, they ensure that everyone is still 'on board'. They like working on projects that can make a difference to others.

> ▶ *Ben is an architect in a small architects' bureau. They mainly build houses, although in recent times they have also constructed a number of school buildings. Ben works on every project as though he is designing and building for himself. He believes that this must be the starting point for every architect. Above all, he likes to work with clients who actively participate in the design process. He does not see it as a problem if those clients put forward plenty of ideas of their own. On the contrary: the more ideas there are, the richer the end result will be. Of course, he always ensures that this end result is feasible in practice. Ben's design drawings are 100% accurate and highly detailed. He is also concerned about the environment and has trained hard to become an expert in the new energy norms applicable to the construction industry. As a result, he has many good ideas about how these norms can be integrated practically into the buildings he designs. Ben is frequently consulted on these matters by his other colleagues in the office. Instead of offering them ready-made solutions, he always takes the trouble to sit around the table with them, so that they can look together at all the available options. At the end*

of the day, he often drives past the sites where work is in progress, to check that everything is going according to plan. He usually stops to talk with the contractors, if they are present. If there are any problems, they immediately search together to find an answer.

The participative leader – possible pitfalls

- Wanting to please
- Perfectionist
- Aloof (C)
- Over-sensitive
- Doubting
- Conservative

Participative leaders like everyone to feel comfortable with the decisions taken and the solutions agreed. They are sometimes willing to sacrifice the quality of the end result in order to maintain good personal relations with colleagues and stakeholders. They are well aware of the practical requirements that need to be satisfied in order to reach a good solution, but often fail to push hard enough to ensure that these requirements are met. This can lead them to avoid making a decision. The same is true when several different priorities need to be considered: they find it difficult to make choices and set a clear order of what needs to be done first. They are afraid to disappoint others if they say 'no' and become frustrated when they cannot achieve the quality of results they desire. When this happens, they have a tendency to become too involved in minor details and find it hard to focus on priorities and a long-term vision.

For Ben, the most difficult aspect of his job is monitoring the progress of the building work and ensuring its successful completion on time. Some contractors have a correct approach to their work and understand that changes need to be made if Ben's plans have not been implemented properly. These are the contractors that Ben likes to work with. But there are other contractors who dare to cut corners and create difficulties when Ben asks them to carry out adjustments. If this happens, he needs to summon all his courage to insist that the changes are made, but he seldom feels comfortable doing this and it costs him a huge amount of energy. If the truth be told, it is not always necessary for him to go into as much detail as he does, but he can't help himself. He thinks it is unprofessional to show his clients plans that are full of scribbled notes and hand-written amendments. Sometimes clients want a truly visionary and artistic design for their home, but Ben is unable to help them and prefers to pass them on to one of his more innovative colleagues. For Ben, a house certainly needs to be attractive, but he also believes firmly that form must follow function. He is not interested in what he regards as architectural frivolities.

Extrovert	iNtuition	Thinking	
In public	Innovative	Formal	
Speaking	Abstract	Analytical	
Thinking while speaking	Inventive	Detached	
Group interaction	Focused on the future	Convincing	
Multi-tasking	Visionary	Competitive	
Flamboyant	Broad view	Discussion	
Action-oriented	Improvisation	Direct	
Outspoken	Ideas	Objective	
Daring	Variation	Task-oriented	
Decide quickly	Fluctuating tempo	Processes and systems	

▶ Figure 14. **Possible points for development for a participative leader**

Strategic leadership – IST

Introvert	Sensing	Thinking
Behind the scenes	Traditional	Formal
Listening	Factual	Analytical
Thinking then speaking	Realistic	Detached
One-to-one conversation	Focused on the present	Convincing
Single-tasking	Operational	Competitive
Reserved	Detail-oriented	Discussion
Plan-oriented	Procedures and rules	Direct
Thoughtful	Practical	Objective
Careful	Routine	Task-oriented
Consider, then decide	Steady tempo	Processes and systems

▶ Figure 15. **The strategic leader**

Characteristics
- Leader-expert
- Tactical
- Calm
- Detailed
- Precise
- Substantiated – 'measuring is knowing'

The strengths of a strategic leader

Strategic leaders are calm and precise. Their leadership is based on their excellent level of expertise. Their approach to their work is logical, thorough and well substantiated, and they pay great attention to detail. When making decisions, they are governed by the facts and by an objective analysis of the advantages and disadvantages of the possible solutions. They perform their duties conscientiously and with a minimum of fuss, whilst giving others considerable freedom to contribute in their own way. They remain cool at all times, even in heated situations, and invariably find a logical and practical solution. They maintain and even increase their level of effort until the desired results are achieved. They are open to the opinions and input of others, providing they are well founded and help to move things forwards.

> *Sophie is a maths teacher in a local secondary school. In addition to giving lessons, in recent years she has also been involved in the digitalisation of education in her school. In this context, she has followed a number of training courses and visited various other schools to see how they have approached the relevant challenges. Following this, last year Sophie drew up a plan for her own school's approach. She described in detail the steps that needed to be taken each year, including the financial investment and the training of staff and pupils that would be necessary. Her plan also included instruments to measure the level of stakeholder satisfaction with each year's progress. For Sophie, it is important that computers become an advanced tool to help teachers and pupils, and not a complicated technical labyrinth in which no one can find their way. Some teachers are not enthusiastic about digitalisation – 'What's wrong with a blackboard and chalk?' – but Sophie is able to reassure them by patiently explaining the support that will be available. In her own calm and determined way, she is gradually leading her school into the digital world of the 21st century...*

The strategic leader – possible pitfalls
- Inflexible
- Perfectionist
- Interrogating (C)
- Insensitive
- Doubting
- Conservative

Strategic leaders are not interested in groundbreaking or revolutionary solutions. They prefer solutions that have already proven their value and have no time for wild ideas. They prefer to work alone and can find it difficult if others try to 'interfere' with what they are doing, especially if these others know less about the matter in hand (which is frequently the case). Strategic leaders can sometimes get lost in detail and lose sight of the bigger picture. They focus primarily on facts and are not interested in what other people think about their approach. As a result, they are often irritated if others fail to follow their clear and logical guidelines. They regard this more emotional response to situations as 'irrational' and of little use in helping to contribute towards practical solutions. Lastly, they do not like to be rushed and will seek to reassert their power and regain attention by asking highly critical questions, if they feel that people are not taking sufficient account of their position.

> For Sophie, the most difficult aspect of her job is dealing with colleagues who make ill-considered suggestions about how the school should be computerised. Some of these colleagues put forward well-meaning proposals for 'flashy' software that is still in the experimental stage. When Sophie presses them for details about the technological reliability of this software and how it will be used in practice, things suddenly go quiet... This is usually enough for Sophie to dismiss the proposals out of hand, but she never stops to think that this reaction might be seen by others as being cool and insensitive, which in turn might affect the enthusiasm of her colleagues for her own digitalisation plans. She recently explained these plans to a full staff meeting. Afterwards, she learnt that some of the teachers were still uneasy about her ideas and were worried that they might not be able to work with the new methods of teaching, even after training. Sophie finds these reactions difficult to understand. Her training plan is clear, complete and well considered. So what have they got to worry about? It is all so unnecessary! Even so, Sophie is asked by the school board to provide additional guidance sessions for these teachers. This irritates her, because it disrupts her planning completely, which is the last thing she has time for at the moment...

Everyone Can Lead

Extrovert		iNtuition		Feeling	
In public		Innovative		Personal	
Speaking		Abstract		Considerate	
Thinking while speaking		Inventive		Engaged	
Group interaction		Focused on the future		Receptive	
Multi-tasking		Visionary		Amenable	
Flamboyant		Broad view		Harmony	
Action-oriented		Improvisation		Tactful	
Outspoken		Ideas		Subjective	
Daring		Variation		Relation-oriented	
Decide quickly		Fluctuating tempo		Culture	

▶ Figure 16. **Possible points for development for a strategic leader**

Visionary leadership – INT

Introvert		iNtuition		Thinking	
Behind the scenes		Innovative		Formal	
Listening		Abstract		Analytical	
Thinking then speaking		Inventive		Detached	
One-to-one conversation		Focused on the future		Convincing	
Single-tasking		Visionary		Competitive	
Reserved		Broad view		Discussion	
Plan-oriented		Improvisation		Direct	
Thoughtful		Ideas		Objective	
Careful		Variation		Task-oriented	
Consider, then decide		Fluctuating tempo		Processes and systems	

▶ Figure 17. **The visionary leader**

Characteristics

- Creative
- Logical
- Determined
- Focused
- Efficient
- Scenario thinker

The strength of the visionary leader

Visionary leaders are focused and determined. They combine their expertise and intuition to develop an inspirational and creative vision for the future. This vision and the wisdom it embodies allows them to win the confidence of others. Their approach is innovative and inventive. When making decisions, they focus on the potential of a solution and the advantages it might bring for the future. They do their work conscientiously and with a minimum of fuss. They have an entrepreneurial frame of mind and are fiercely determined. They are good scenario thinkers and can quickly assess the potential benefits and pitfalls of any situation or approach. They try to move others in the direction that leads to the realisation of their vision and they do this in a persistent but respectful manner.

> Miguel is a senior engineer for the national railways. He has many years of experience behind him and nowadays he is the man they call in whenever there is a serious problem that threatens to disrupt the train service. The first thing he does on these occasions is to investigate the cause and then assess all the possible solutions. There is no one better than Miguel at creating order out the mass of technical information that needs to be analysed in these situations. After a thorough evaluation, he unfailingly selects the right approach. This might sound easy, but it is not. Every situation is different and there is no manual with a set of 'standard' solutions from which he can choose. Each time the puzzle is different and he needs all his technical know-how to find the right answers. He can see all the connections that will lead not only to the most efficient but also to the safest way forward. Having made his decision, he then explains to his colleagues exactly what steps need to be taken. He supervises them to make sure that everything is carried out in the right order and is properly co-ordinated. While he is doing all this, Miguel does not like

> *to be disturbed. He needs his full focus and concentration to be certain that the solution is correctly implemented. Minor obstacles seldom worry him; his technical knowledge is so great that he can easily find suitable alternatives to deal with them. Once the main problem has been resolved and the trains are running again, Miguel also has the foresight to organise the replacement of his 'emergency' measures with a more permanent solution.*

The visionary leader – possible pitfalls

- Inflexible
- Dreamer
- Interrogating (C)
- Insensitive
- Doubting
- Easily bored

Visionary leaders like to work on their own, at their own speed and following their own agenda. They have a huge dislike for bureaucratic procedures, especially if they have not been properly thought through or serve (in their eyes) no useful purpose. They are business-like and always get straight to the point. They have no interest in small talk and polite conversation, which they regard as a waste of valuable time, and they take little account of the feelings of others. They are fascinated by the visionary aspect of the solutions they develop, which, in their opinion, must be sufficient to persuade everyone to jump on the bandwagon. However, they are sometimes so occupied with this visionary aspect that they have little interest in the practical details that are necessary to realise the vision. To make matters worse, they often think so quickly that others are not able to follow. If they need to put down their ideas on paper, they focus purely on the essence of the message they wish to convey. As a result, they sometimes combine different concepts and ideas in a single sentence, the meaning of which is not always clear to everyone. Leaders of this kind seem super-confident, because they seldom express any doubts.

For Miguel, the most difficult aspect of his job is the countless procedures and rules issued by the national rail company. He understands that these have been introduced to guarantee the safety and reliability of the rail service, but they do not make his work any easier. If he needs to intervene to solve a serious technical problem, he feels that these rules and procedures should no longer apply. In fact, they often actually prevent him from doing what he needs to do, so he finds his own alternatives to get around them, whilst still maintaining the necessary levels of safety and reliability. At such moments, it is better not to disturb Miguel. He needs time and space to assess all the possible solutions and their implications. Once he has found the best of these solutions, he communicates his conclusions to those who need to know, who then send out the necessary maintenance teams to do the actual repair work. Over the years, Miguel has learnt that his instructions need to be clear, preferably with step-by-step explanations, so that nothing is overlooked or forgotten. He continues to monitor everything that is happening, but without getting bogged down in the details. Miguel is well respected by his colleagues for his expertise, but no one really knows him as a person. Most people find him to be cool and distant. After the problem has been solved, he is happy to discuss what lessons for the future can be learnt from the incident, but he has no interest in a friendly chat that is not work-related. Instead, he prefers to be alone, because that is how he finds it easiest to decompress after the stress of an intervention.

Extrovert		Sensing		Feeling	
In public		Traditional		Personal	
Speaking		Factual		Considerate	
Thinking while speaking		Realistic		Engaged	
Group interaction		Focused on the present		Receptive	
Multi-tasking		Operational		Amenable	
Flamboyant		Detail-oriented		Harmony	
Action-oriented		Procedures and rules		Tactful	
Outspoken		Practical		Subjective	
Daring		Routine		Relation-oriented	
Decide quickly		Steady tempo		Culture	

▶ Figure 18. **Possible points for development for a visionary leader**

Beliefs

Beliefs play a crucial role in 'bringing out the best in yourself and in others'. For example, limiting beliefs can prevent or hinder you from becoming the best possible version of yourself. In this next section we will examine various limiting beliefs that may be applicable to you and look at how you can convert them into empowering beliefs.

First and foremost, it is important that you are able to identify and recognise limiting beliefs. Beliefs, including limiting beliefs, often start with the following words:

- I may not / I am not allowed to...
- I must (always)...
- I find it difficult to ...
- Everything must (always)...
- Others have to...
- Others are not allowed to...
- I am...
- I am always...
- I am never...
- I am not...
- I cannot...
- I can never...
- I always want...
- I never want...
- Others are (often / never)...

As an exercise, try completing the above sentences. Fill them in intuitively with the first thing that comes to mind, without too much prior thinking. The sentences can often be completed in different ways, so just write down everything that pops into your head.

If you are not comfortable with this way of working, as an alternative you can find below a list of many of the most common limiting beliefs. Indicate alongside each of them the extent to which you think they are applicable to you:

- 10 = always
- ...
- 5 = sometimes
- ...
- 0 = never

If appropriate, you can supplement Figure 19 with limiting beliefs that you can identify in yourself but are not already included in the list.

Limiting belief	Score
I can't make any mistakes.	
I always have to know everything in my field.	
Others have to like me.	
I must always take everyone into account.	
I must always be bright and cheerful.	
Everything always has to be done honestly / fairly.	
I must meet the expectations of others.	
I must avoid conflict.	
I must always have everything under control.	
I must always give 100%.	
I can never say 'no' to my… (manager, colleagues, partner, children, customers, etc.).	
I must always be there for my … (colleagues, children, parents, partner, etc.).	
I must be more ambitious for … (greater responsibility, a better job, etc.).	
There must be a solution for every problem.	
I am responsible for everything that happens to me.	
Every decision must be based on logical facts.	
I must always help others with their problems.	

▶ Figure 19. **What score do you give yourself for these limiting beliefs?**

Dig deeper: what is the real limiting belief?

Once you have mapped out your limiting beliefs in this way, dig deeper to see what fundamental beliefs they conceal. Consider, for example, 'I can never say "no" to my colleagues'. What really lies behind this belief? It might be an underlying fear: 'My colleagues will think that I am not friendly/helpful'. Or at an ever deeper level: 'I am afraid that they won't like me any more'. And even deeper: 'Soon I will be completely isolated at work'. In other words, your fundamental belief is: 'If I say "no" to my colleagues at work, I am afraid that I will soon find myself completely isolated'. There is often a fear of this kind hidden behind a belief. These are the fears that you need to identify.

How do your limiting beliefs limit you?

We acquire our beliefs from our parents, education, upbringing and other environments, but also as a result of certain life experiences. These beliefs, even the limiting ones, will have helped you at some point in the past, but is that still the case today? Re-examine your list of limiting beliefs by looking at them from the opposite perspective. How have these beliefs already imposed limits on you? What opportunities have they caused you to miss? What would your life look like if you were not held back by these limitations? Imagine that you hold a completely opposite set of beliefs: what would your life look like then? Try to make the answers to these questions specific and give examples.

How can you replace your limiting beliefs with empowering beliefs?

If you discover that a limiting belief is preventing you from reaching your goal and/or from living and working the way you want, you need to replace it with an empowering belief. This will not happen overnight, so be realistic and at first take small steps in the right direction. Beliefs are often stubborn and difficult to change. Trying to go from one extreme to the other in a single leap will inevitably lead to disappointment. You can only transform limiting beliefs into empowering ones by a phased approach.

To start this process, it is first necessary to be aware of your limiting beliefs. As a result of the above exercises, you should already have a good idea of what they are and also what underlying fundamental fears they represent.

In a second stage, you need to identify situations in which these limiting beliefs occur. Let us look again at the limiting belief 'If I say "no" at work, I am afraid that I will soon find myself completely isolated'. When does this happen? Does it always happen? Or is it only with certain colleagues? Or is it only with certain requests from certain colleagues? At the end of this self-questioning, you may conclude that you are not afraid to say 'no' to certain colleagues in one-on-one situations and when your agenda is already full, but are only afraid to say 'no' when other colleagues are present and your agenda is not full. In this way, you should be able to establish when you are most likely to be confronted by limiting beliefs, so that you can devote the necessary attention to dealing with them effectively and transforming them into empowering beliefs.

How exactly? This transformation takes place in two distinct and equally important steps.

Step 1: Make a list of what it will mean for you if you are able to complete this transformation successfully. What advantages would it bring? In our 'afraid to say no' example, this might be:
- I will be able to keep my amount of work to a realistic level, so that I can:
  - deliver the best possible quality;
  - keep my existing promises (to my other colleagues / my boss);
  - keep my weekends free from work;
  - avoid overworking, which will allow me more time for my partner / family / friends.
- I will be able to concentrate on the tasks that are really important (to me, to the organisation, etc.).
- I will be able to avoid doing work for which I am not the most suitable person.
- I will be able to avoid unnecessary stress and take better care of my health.
- I will be able to say 'no' to unimportant activities, which means saying 'yes' to important activities.
  (This almost brings us to a new and empowering belief.)
- ...

Step 2: Challenge your limiting belief. Test it to see if the current situation is really the way you think it is. You can do this by again asking various questions. In our example, these questions might include: 'Do you think that someone is not being a good colleague if he or she says "no"?' Or: 'Has someone ever said to you that you are not being a good colleague when you have said "no"?' Or: 'Have you seen any of your colleagues get angry when others have said "no"?' You can also try to look at things from the opposite point of view. For example: 'My colleagues will be pleased if I say "no", because it will also make it easier for them to say "no" when they are also too busy'. Or: 'My colleagues will be pleased that I have dared to set a boundary, because they now realise that they should do the same thing'.

This questioning process should not only give you a different insight into the situation but also the motivation to act on that insight. In this way, you might eventually reach the conclusion that a well-founded reason for saying 'no' might actually result in your colleagues feeling greater respect for you, rather than feeling angry or frustrated. In this case, your new empowering belief might be: 'Saying "no" when there is a good reason to say "no" helps me to focus on what is important and wins me the respect of my colleagues'. If it is possible for you to see what you can gain through empowering beliefs, this makes it much easier to put them into practice.

This final phase of applying the new beliefs in practice can also be implemented step by step, so that you proceed towards the desired new approach gradually. Do not immediately start saying 'no' to difficult or dominant colleagues, or when discussing a sensitive subject. Start carefully with friendly colleagues and routine matters. In this way, you can systematically build up confidence and start to experience that your new belief really works. You already know the situations in which the old limiting belief is likely to arise – at meetings, during certain activities, even at the coffee machine, etc. – so be extra-careful when dealing with these situations. Think consciously about how you apply your new belief. Seek out the colleagues who are most likely to give you a helping hand or a push in the back when you need it.

Within the context of leadership, you need to search in particular for limiting beliefs that prevent you from bringing out the best in yourself and in others. What is stopping you from showing your best side? What is stopping you from inspiring others to bring out the best in themselves? How can you replace those limiting beliefs with empowering beliefs?

Knowing what you want

For many people, knowing what you want is the most difficult question of all. The answer can be influenced by countless different factors: your personality, your values, your needs and beliefs, your dreams and ideals, the expectations of your environment, your skills and competencies, etc. In an organisational context, you also need to find the right balance and fit between your personal objectives and those of the organisation you work for.

Knowing what you want is closely connected with our definition of leadership as 'a process of self-insight and positive influencing with the aim of bringing out the best in yourself and in others, in order to achieve the objectives of the organisation'. This raises two questions. What do you want to bring to the surface in yourself? What do you want to bring to the surface in others? You are the only person who can answer these questions. You are the only person who can decide and define what you want.

Knowing what you want is crucial for taking the right decisions in life. It determines the things to which you say 'yes' and the things to which you say 'no'. It is a compass that helps to guide you in the right direction. In addition, knowing what you want helps to bring meaning and purpose into your life. Why am I here on this planet? How do I want to make a difference? Having a purpose helps you to keep going when the going gets tough. Last but not least, it is important to know what you want, so that you can be certain that you always respect your own wishes and priorities and not the – imposed – wishes and priorities of others.

Your farewell speech

A classic career exercise that I often ask people to perform, as a way to identify their goals in life and at work, is to write the farewell speech that they would like to hear someone give when they retire or at their funeral. This may sound a bit dark at first, but it can actually be highly illuminating. Who would you like to give the speech? And what would you like to hear them say about you? It is an exercise for which you need to make the necessary time, so that you can think calmly and quietly about what you want to write, before setting it down on paper. When you read it back, you will probably find that it says less about what you achieved and more about who you were. It will contain phrases like: 'He was a true bon vivant' and not 'He had the most fantastic collection of fine wines'. Or: 'He was a passionate business leader' and not 'His company achieved an annual turnover of more than xxx million euros'.

Values and needs

Leaders honour their core values, but they are *flexible* in how they execute them. Colin Powell

The 'why' question is hugely important if you wish to discover what you truly want. If you have a goal in your life, why do you have that goal? Imagine that your dream is to start your own business. Why is that your dream? What is there in that dream that makes it so important to you? Do you want your own company so that you can make your own decisions (= freedom?)? Or for the challenge it presents (= testing yourself?)? Or to earn lots of money (= financial security?)? Or to provide people with jobs (= helping others?)? Let's take another example. Imagine now that your ambition is to be rich. Why? So I can buy an expensive car. Why? Because they are such good fun to drive (= pleasure?). Or because people will look up to me (= recognition?) Or because I will be able to attract the man/

woman of my dreams (= affection?). Once you find that you cannot take your 'why' question any further, you will probably have discovered one of your fundamental values or needs. In the above example, this means that your fundamental need is not 'I would like to be rich', but 'I would like some pleasure / recognition / affection'.

This is a useful way to learn more about your values and needs, and to identify the ones that are most important to you. As you can see, in the examples above I have always put a question mark next to the value. Why? Because values are highly personal. You might think that having a challenge in life is an important need, whereas others might have no such need. In short: you are the only person who can determine the values and needs that really matter to you. Figure 20 is a list of some of the most common values and needs. You can use this list to identify the ones that are personally important to you. By asking the 'why' question, you will discover which of these values and needs are fundamental. Once you know this, you can start to think about how you can implement them in both your professional and private lives. This will then become your personal mission: what you want to achieve and why you want to achieve it.

Indicate in the list below the extent to which the values and needs are already present in your life and the way(s) in which they can be fulfilled through your work for your organisation. Why this emphasis on work? Because work is the context for the story of this book. For this reason, values that are not yet fully present in your life but can be more completely fulfilled through your work are the ones on which you should focus most attention in this present exercise.

	Value or need	Importance 10 = very important 0 = not important	Is already present 10 = fully 0 = not at all	Can it be fulfilled in my organisation? 10 = many possibilities 0 = no possibility	Action point for me? Yes / No
1	Action				
2	Affection				
3	Variation				
4	Autonomy				
5	Balance				
6	Competence				
7	Comfort				
8	Competition				
9	Creativity				
10	Simplicity				
11	Recognition				
12	Ethics				
13	Happiness				
14	Health				
15	Growth				
16	Harmony				
17	Helpfulness				
18	Integrity				
19	Influence				
20	Social usefulness				
21	Order				
22	Pleasure				
23	Respect				

24	Fame			
25	Calm			
26	Collaboration			
27	Beauty			
28	Solidarity			
29	Status			
30	Challenge			
31	Progress			
32	Joy			
33	Friendship			
34	Prosperity			
35	Wisdom			
36	Certainty			
37	Self-respect			
38	Self-confidence			
39	Meaning			
40	Caring			
41				
42				
43				
44				
45				

▶ Figure 20. **Which values and needs are important to you?**

Make a list of the top ten values and needs that are most important to you. Describe what each of these values and needs means to you. If it helps, you can split a single value/norm into two separate values/norms or, alternatively, you can combine two values/norms to create a single value/norm. Here are a few examples of what I mean:

- Caring: I want to support people during emotionally challenging periods in their life by listening to them and helping them in their search to find answers and solutions.

- Fame: I want to be internationally respected in my field and consulted worldwide for my superior expertise.

- Harmony and wisdom: I want to work in a stimulating environment where, through the people with whom I work, I will be able to gain new insights that can help me to find and maintain personal balance.

- Variation and collaboration: I like to frequently change from one work environment to another, so that I can continually learn and implement new tasks in collaboration with others.

This exercise will give you a good indication of the things that are important to you; in other words, the things that you want out of life. Check to see how far they are already present/fulfilled and how this process can be further extended through your work for your organisation. This summary will give you a basis for your approach to your work and for setting the right priorities: what are the things you want to do that will allow you to bring out the best in yourself and in others?

The roles in your life

Another way to know what you want is to look at how you want to make a difference in the world. A difference for yourself, but also – and often primarily – for others. In my experience, this is an exercise that can help many people to discover what they want in a most pragmatic way. You start by making a summary of the different roles that you have in your life: partner, parent, child, friend, employee, citizen, member of a society or club, neighbour, etc. For each of these roles you then need to define what you want to achieve and how will you achieve it. This will result in sentences that have a structure similar to the following:

I WANT (WHO) (ACTION), SO THAT (DESIRED RESULT).

Here are a few examples:
- as a barista: I want to prepare the best possible coffee for my customers, so that I can give them a moment of pleasure and enjoyment during their busy working day.
- as a cleaner: I want to clean the office premises thoroughly each night, so that each morning the employees of our organisation can start work with renewed pleasure and enthusiasm.
- as a car mechanic: I want to give the customers of our garage well maintained cars, so that they and their passengers can drive in comfort and safety.
- as banker: I want to give our customers the most appropriate investment advice, so that the money they invest has the best possible chance to produce the level of return they expect.

If you want, you can also further sub-divide the various roles:
- as a parent -> as a parent of Hannah and as a parent of Noah
- as a friend -> as a friend of Michael, Paula, Alex, etc.

This is particularly useful for your role as an employee in an organisation:
- as a colleague of Jessica, Jacob, Mia, etc.
- as a team member of the IT team, the sales team, etc.
- as the manager of David, Lea, etc.
- as the direct reporting officer of Julia, Paul, etc.

Here are some examples of what people might want in these kinds of organisational contexts:
- I want to help the IT team by facilitating their consultation with others, so that we can reach the best possible decisions.
- I want to make time for my colleague John, so that I can help him with his presentation.

- I want to share my vision with the management, so that I can contribute towards improved results for the organisation.
- I want to boost the self-confidence of my colleague Elsie, by regularly giving her compliments about her good work.
- I want to make maximum use of the potential of everyone in my team, by defining roles and responsibilities as clearly as possible.
- I want to lend a helping hand to my colleagues in the warehouse during busy periods, to prevent them from being overworked.
- I want to bring more structure into the meetings of our project team, so that we can make better and more broadly based decisions.

In this way, you should arrive at a series of things that you want, which should be compatible with our definition of leadership as 'a process of self-insight and positive influencing with the aim of bringing out the best in yourself and in others, in order to achieve the objectives of the organisation'. By looking at your organisation and at all the people you work with, you will be able to determine how, by bringing out the best in yourself (action), you can help to bring out the best (desired result) in others (who).

Positive influencing

Objectives and priorities

> **Leadership** is about making others *better* as a result of your presence and making sure that impact lasts in *our absence*. Sheryl Sandberg

Now that we have examined the processes of self-insight and, consequently, have a better understanding of how we can (and want to) bring out the best in ourselves, it is time to explore the other part of our definition of leadership: bringing out the best in others. This will involve us looking at the concept of positive influencing as a means to accomplish this goal for the purpose of achieving the objectives of the organisation. To do this, we first need to determine and define the specific end result that we wish to attain. As Stephen Covey so tellingly put it in his bestseller *The 7 Habits of Highly Effective People*: 'Start with the end in mind'. Determining and/or having control over your destination before you start your journey is an absolute must.

It may sound like common sense to say that you need to know what you want to achieve before you start any task or activity, but it is surprising how often people fail to do this. Just think of all the times you have sat in a meeting and asked yourself what its purpose is supposed to be. Was it intended to convey information? Or to reach a decision? Or to generate new ideas? Or to ask for advice? Often you won't have a clue! All you know is that it seemed to last for a very long time without reaching any obvious conclusion. So whatever you are doing, whether it is a consultation exercise or a practical task, it is always a good idea to decide upon the exact purpose of your activity in advance. You will be amazed how often there is no clear and obvious answer.

Once you know your end goal, the 'why' question is often a useful second question to ask. This will allow you to discover if and how your goal contributes to the wider objectives of the organisation. Only then will you know if you are heading in the right direction. This has the added advantage of making clear the usefulness and value of your work. The 'why' question also helps you to see what the route to your end goal should look like. Imagine (in a non-organisational context) that your objective is 'to walk 5 kilometres'. In this case, various different answers to the 'why' question are possible: to improve your fitness (in which case you need to pick a physically challenging route and walk as quickly as possible); to enjoy the delights of nature (in which case you need to choose a quieter, calmer route that you will walk more slowly); or to visit sites of interest along the way (in which case you can ask yourself whether or not walking is the best option and might it not be better to go by bike or car). In other words, the 'why' question can often help to show you the best way to reach your destination or, on occasion, can even prompt you to question that destination.

The 'why' question automatically brings you to the ultimate key questions: what is the reason behind the end goal and is this, in fact, the right goal? Or to express it in slightly different terms: is the end goal the right answer to the reason or the problem that lies at its root? Many end goals often seek to deal with the symptoms of an underlying problem, without tackling the problem itself. You can compare it with taking an aspirin for a headache, but ignoring the fact that the headache is actually caused by stress. What you really should be doing is attempting to remove the cause of that stress. The speed at which society and organisations move in today's world means that we often opt for the fast and curative treatment of symptoms – a quick fix – rather than concentrating on the preventative solution of problems. Unfortunately, quick fix solutions often turn out to be quick-and-dirty solutions. I am not denying that they have their uses in organisations, especially in emergency situations, but you need to be aware that they are not a fundamental and lasting answer to your problems.

It is also necessary to have a clear understanding about the cost, speed and quality of the end goal that you wish to realise. People often expect that objectives will be accomplished as quickly as possible, with as few resources as possible and to the highest possible standard of quality. Unfortunately, these three elements do not go together very often. If you can satisfy two of the elements, the third one usually suffers as a result. Fast and cheap generally leads to poor quality. Fast and high quality costs a lot of money. And achieving high quality with a low budget always takes lots of time. It is a good idea to know which of these three possibilities you intend to adopt before starting out on your journey. The route that you take to your destination will be very different in all three cases, depending on the priorities you set.

The clearer your goal and your priorities, the easier it is to attune your input and approach to the results that you want to achieve. Imagine, for example, that quality is the priority and that by nature you are a very precise and accurate person. This scenario will allow you to use your natural preferences and talents to the full. If, however, speed is the priority, in this scenario you will need to be flexible. Of course, you can still keep a watchful eye over the quality, but you will have to do this in a manner that does not have a negative impact on the speed that is now deemed to be more important. This is where the creativity of Authentic Adaptability begins.

Adaptability

The context

Authentic Adaptability is a kind of balancing act. You need to find the right balance between remaining true to your own personal preferences (what you like to do and are good at doing, what you want and who you are) and adjusting to the context. A context that involves putting out a fire demands a different approach to providing care and assistance to the victims of a traffic accident, which in turn requires a different approach to carrying out a fire prevention check, and so on.

A number of leadership models share this insight. In these cases, reference is often made to situational leadership. One of the most well known of these models is the situational leadership model devised by Hersey and Blanchard. This model has just two dimensions: the level of motivation and the level of competence of the person you are leading. This results in four possible situations: not competent and not motivated; not competent but motivated; competent but not motivated; competent and motivated. The model explains which manner of leadership is best for each of these four situations.

In The Leadership Connection, however, I will argue that there are more dimensions that have a defining effect on the context. Of these, the following dimensions are the most important:

The person(s) involved
It is not only a question of what the other person knows and is able to do. It is equally a question of who this person is and what he wants and needs. For example, working with someone who is extremely impatient and always wants to be in the spotlight, but does not yet have all the necessary skills, is very different from working with someone who has the patience of a saint and prefers to stay in the background, even though he is already highly skilled.

The nature of the activity
Different kinds of activities require different styles of leadership. Co-ordinating a scientific research project at a university is not the same as co-ordinating a police

raid on a criminal gang. Collaborating to set up a technical installation is different from collaborating to conduct a lobbying campaign.

The timing

Activities and projects pass through different phases, from start via implementation to completion. Each of these phases places different emphases in terms of the kind of leadership required. Leading the initial brainstorming session that gets a project off the ground involves different skills than leading the final completion and transfer meeting with the client at the end of the project.

The (organisational) culture

'Culture eats strategy for breakfast' is a famous statement by Peter Drucker, which underlines the tremendous impact that culture can have on organisations. Whereas in one (organisational) culture it might be seen as a strength if the leader's ideas are challenged in public, in another organisation this same behaviour might be a 'career limiting move'!

The circumstances

Where you are and who is present can also have an important influence on determining the most appropriate style of leadership. The way a politician addresses his fellow party members at a conference – and therefore in the presence of the public and the press – will be very different from the way he addresses those same party members in the privacy of the party's headquarters.

In short, the context will always help to determine the most appropriate style of leadership in any given situation. Being able to read the context is therefore one of the most important and most universal leadership skills. Moreover, it is a skill that most people are able to acquire over the years, involving quite some trial and error.

Reading the context

You now have a clear insight about the objectives that need to be attained. You also know the correct order of priorities in relation to cost, quality and time. These are excellent starting points from which to further assess the context.

Listening and asking questions

In many organisations you are expected to make quick decisions and take prompt action. The temptation is to immediately jump into solution mode, without stopping to analyse the context thoroughly. Before you know it, everyone is moving off in different directions. This is not a good idea. In the end, faster is often slower and slower is usually faster. Or to put it in slightly different terms: if you invest more time at the beginning on a good analysis of the objectives and the context, in the long run you will save time and achieve the desired results more quickly. Listening and asking questions is the simplest and easiest way to gain better insight into the context. If you know what everyone thinks about the best way to achieve the objectives, you will immediately have a good overview of people's preferences and the contributions they wish to make. This will allow you to decide how and where you can create the most added value. You can compare it with fitting together the pieces of a puzzle. You first need to look at the separate pieces that people have already laid on the table, so that you can decide which missing pieces you need to fill in. Imagine, for example, that 'creativity', 'passion' and 'technical expertise' are already present. This will help you to see that 'teamwork', 'quality', 'coordination', 'motivation', etc. still need to be added to the total mix.

Observing

When you ask questions and listen, it is not only important to note the content of what is being said; you also need to observe the way in which that content is expressed. Who reacted with irritation or with enthusiasm, and to which questions? Who seemed passionate about which ideas? Who listened cautiously or even sceptically, and to which arguments? How and when did people give voice to their own vision? Who was slumped disinterestedly in his chair and who sat excitedly on the edge of his seat? Who was listening to others and who was interested primarily in airing his own ideas? Who agreed with who and who disagreed with who? In this way, you can put together a picture of the likes and dislikes of everyone in your team and can see how these likes and dislikes interact. Use all your empathy and your emotional and social intelligence to identify which emotions are at play. This will allow you to search for what motivates people and to identify what they want to achieve. Who wants to convince everyone else that their vision is the right one? Who wants to move ahead quickly? Who wants to control everything? Who asks critical questions? Who wants to launch new ideas? Who is clearly not interested in the project? Who wants to gain prestige from the project, and how? Who believes or does not believe in the objectives and/or the approach?

Points of contact

Observe everyone's behaviour and try to estimate what underlying beliefs, preferences, values, needs and motivations this behaviour conceals. Do not set the bar too high for yourself. Even experienced psychologists are unable to 'decode' everyone in the blink of an eye! Use the model that you used for yourself in the chapter on 'Self-insight' to now assess others. Bear in mind that everyone is unique and that you will never be able to paint the full picture. But that is not really necessary. The most important thing is to find points of contact that will allow you to make a connection with the people you work with. You can do this by searching for common beliefs, preferences, values, needs and/or motives. For example, you might share with someone the same need for making a thorough analysis; or a preference for systematic follow-up; or a motivating passion to put innovative ideas into practice; or the value of treating every member of the team with respect; or the belief that mutual trust is the key to success. This is what I mean when I speak of points of contact. Via these points of contact you will be able to make connections with others.

As soon as a connection exists, you will be able to bring your own unique competencies, values, needs, beliefs, preferences and motivations into your work. Imagine that you are working with a colleague and that you both share the same motivation to provide top-quality results. That is the point of contact that creates the connection between you. Let's now further imagine that your colleague has a preference for reaching your shared objective through the careful step-by-step planning of all the relevant activities, whereas your preference is to carefully check and re-check everything a final time when the work is completed. By combining these different methods, the two of you become complementary. In this way, you bring out the best in yourself, but you also bring out the best in the other. Another example? You might share a passion for innovation with a colleague. Your colleague devotes his attention to converting innovation into a realistic plan of approach, whereas your attention is focused on getting other members of the team to support the innovation wholeheartedly. The point of contact is innovation and you are complementary in terms of 'developing a realistic plan' and 'getting the support of the team'.

The more flexibly you can adjust your own style, the easier you will find it to connect with people of a different style. If one of your colleagues has a need for substantiated proof before acting, provide him with the facts and figures he wants. If another colleague is anxious to make progress quickly, give him a list of powerful action points. Someone else wants to share his concerns about certain aspects of the project? Listen sympathetically to what he has to say. In other words, you first look to see what is important to others in terms of their values, needs, preferences, beliefs and motivation, and then you try to accommodate them as far as you reasonably can. If you have observed them closely, you will probably find that there will be at least one and possibly more points of contact. The likelihood that you will have no points of contact is relatively small. Try to make a connection with everyone involved, but without playing a role that you do not really mean. That is the key to Adaptable Authenticity.

You can even create new points of contact, but this will only be possible with the right motivation. This means that you need to know what is important for you and why. If you really want something and if you know yourself thoroughly, you can always make a new quality or characteristic your own. For example, if, by nature, you are a bad listener (until recently, listening was not important to you), but from now on you want to find the best solution for problems by listening to the ideas of others, you can still develop the required listening skills but you must do so in a manner that is credible and sincere. In other words: authentic. Not some contrived (fake) listening technique that you have learned from a book, but your own honest and genuine way of listening to others.

From time to time, it may happen that you have such a dislike for a particular belief, motivation, value need or preference that it is impossible to connect with the other person, even if other points of contact exist. Sometimes, the difference between you is just too great to be bridged. Perhaps you are confronted with someone who fails to treat others with respect, which is something you cannot tolerate under any circumstances. In situations of this kind, it is important to be honest with yourself and not to go against your own feelings. If you do, you will end up having to fake your behaviour, which will inevitably lead to a loss of trust and disconnection. It can sometimes help to name your dislikes and make them discussable, but these are often sensitive issues, especially if you are dealing with characteristics or beliefs that are deeply rooted in either yourself or the others involved. To resolve this, you need to be an adept of Leadership 2.0 or, even higher! So think very carefully before deciding to follow this route.

Adapting to the context

Authentic adaptability implies that you adapt your actions and behaviour to match the context, but in a natural way, a way that is truly your own. You take as your starting point the organisational objectives that need to be achieved. These objectives might be objectives for you personally or for the team or department to which you belong. On the basis of the context, you assess what you think is necessary at that moment for you to move in the direction of the objectives. Ultimately, you should use your own judgement to decide this, but there is nothing wrong with also listening to your colleagues, so that you can know what they think is necessary. Go in search of an answer to the question: what is the best approach, given the people involved, the nature of the activity, the timing, the (organisational) culture and the current circumstances?

Once you are convinced that you know the best approach to follow, see if you can and if you want to make a contribution to that approach and, if so, how. In other words, you consciously select from all your different competencies the ones that you think will best contribute towards the approach that will ultimately lead you towards the objectives. Having done this, you then need to apply your Authentic Adaptability: use the competencies you have selected in such a manner that they will be accepted and supported by all the other people involved. This is the flexibility in style that I mentioned earlier. It allows you to make your contribution in a way that will make it easier for others to work with you. To achieve this, you can also make use of points of contact with these others, creating connections that will enable you to make your own unique contribution in your own unique way. Authentic Adaptability requires non-stop effort and practice, day after day. It means that you must constantly be aware of how you would normally react (your natural reflex or habit) and how you can better react in response to the context in which you find yourself.

During the past few days, Bert has been working on a plan for a new project he wants to launch. When making such a plan, Bert is always thorough and detailed in his approach. He thinks of all the necessary actions, the people involved, the necessary time, the likely risks and the possible back-up scenarios. **(This is Bert's talent. He likes doing it and he does it well. It is also in keeping with his natural preference.)** *Today, Bert is going to propose his plan to his boss, Anna, who must give her approval before Bert can go ahead. Bert knows that Anna, like himself, attaches great importance to such projects and their successful completion on time.* **(This is the point of connection between Bert and Anna, the motivation they both share.)** *Bert hopes that Anna will support his project and defend it throughout the organisation. He knows that Anna is a driven, no-nonsense manager who likes to see things move forward quickly.* **(This is Anna's talent. She likes doing it and she does it well. It is also in keeping with her natural preference.)** *Bert is proud of his detailed plan and would like to spend half a day with Anna to run through it step by step.* **(This is the natural preference of Bert, his natural reflex.)** *However, during previous projects he has noticed that Anna is not the most patient person and she is not that interested in all the fine details.* **(Bert has been careful to observe Anna's preferences on previous occasions.)** *As a result, this time he has decided to approach things differently. He has summarised the most important milestones and Anna's role on a single sheet of paper, and has asked her for a meeting of just half an hour to discuss all the key points.* **(This is Authentic Adaptability: Bert has adjusted his approach to reach his objective – Anna's approval and support for his plan – in the most efficient way.)** *Even so, he takes his computer with his detailed planning along to the meeting, just in case there are any specific questions that Anna wishes to raise. Bert starts the meeting by emphasising the importance of successfully completing the project on time.* **(Bert seeks to connect with Anna through a shared point of contact.)** *Thereafter, he takes Anna through his short summary of milestones and explains the role he foresees for her in the project.* **(Bert adapts his style to match Anna's style.)** *Anna thinks that it all looks good and tells Bert that she is confident that he can bring the project to a successful conclusion. She confirms that she will be happy to recommend his project to others in the organisation and will defend it, where necessary.* **(There is trust and a Positive Connection between Bert and Anna, and Bert has ensured that they will both be able to bring out the best in themselves: Bert through the implementation of his detailed plan, Anna through her defence of the plan at the organisational level.)**

Brent and Eva work together on the same production line in a car factory. Like the rest of their team, they are both proud that they work for this top-quality brand. (This is a point of contact between all the members of the team.) It is one of the last brands still producing cars in their country. Brent is specialised in the solving of small technical problems on the production line. His interest in technology and his practical skills make him the ideal person for this job. (This is Brent's talent. He likes doing it and he does it well.) Eva is the quality control manager on the production line. Together with the people in her department, she regularly introduces new processes and procedures to eliminate production malfunctions. She explains the new procedures to everyone, tells them that she expects them to be followed and informs them that regular checks will be carried out. (This is Eva's talent. She likes doing it and she does it well.) In recent weeks, a number of problems have been occurring in a particular section of the production line. Brent has already had to intervene on several occasions, usually at the request of Sarah. Sarah works on this section of the line and is seen by her colleagues in that section as their 'spokesperson'. This is a role that Sarah is happy to take on; she is proud that her colleagues trust her to defend their interests. (This is Sarah's talent. She likes doing it and she does it well.) When Eva learns that there are so many problems on this section of the line, she decides to start an investigation to discover the cause and to see how the problems can be avoided in future. She quickly discovers that a few extra checks at key moments will provide the necessary solution. The next day, she writes out instructions for the new procedures. (This is her preferred way of working: independently and with quality as her objective.) From her previous experience with the introduction of new procedures, she is aware that there can sometimes be resistance, with people complaining about 'not another new way of doing things'. This is not good for the atmosphere on the production line. (Eva has learnt this from past observation; the desire for a positive team atmosphere is a point of connection.) As a result, this time Eva first asks Brent and Sarah to come and discuss the proposed new procedure, so that they can give their feedback. (This is Authentic Adaptability: Eva adjusts her approach and style to the context, so that she is better able to achieve her objectives.) Sarah and Brent are happy to accept Eva's offer of consultation. Brent even has a creative suggestion that will make the procedure simpler and more effective. (Eva brings out the best in Brent.) Now that they are sitting around the same table, Eva decides to push her boundaries still further (Authentic Adaptability frequently *requires you to push your boundaries) and asks if Sarah would be willing to explain the new procedure to her colleagues. This is not easy for Eva to do: usually she prefers to keep all aspects of control and follow-up in her own hands. Sarah agrees to Eva's suggestion, on condition that she gives her the necessary support. (**Eva brings out the best in Sarah.**) Because of the trust and respect that Sarah enjoys with her colleagues (**this is their Positive Connection**), the new procedure is accepted and implemented without difficulty. (**The objective is achieved.**) During the following weeks, Eva carries out a few control checks and sees that everything is being done according to the new guidelines. Brent congratulates her on the improvement and says that he has another technical problem that he would like to discuss with her...* ◄*

THE LEADERSHIP CONNECTION IN ACTION

What kind of leader do you want to be?

Leadership and learning are indispensable to each other. John F. Kennedy

'What kind of leader do you want to be?' is the fundamental question with which your journey with The Leadership Connection begins. This applies to both your personal leadership and hierarchical leadership. What impact do you want to have in your organisation? What contribution do you wish to make? This is a question that searches for meaning and happiness. How, through your work in your organisation, do you want to find meaning in your life and happiness in your job?

As soon as you know the answer to this question, you can then start to look closely at the role you currently play in the organisation and, above all, how you fulfil that role. What impact do you have at the moment and what impact do you want to have in the future? By using the two guiding principles of The Leadership Connection you can build a bridge between your current approach and your desired approach. Taking your personal development in hand in this way is also a form of personal leadership.

In the following section we will search together for the answers to the questions that the two guiding principles of The Leadership Connection require you to ask:

Positive Connection:
- How do I build trust?
- How do I show and earn respect?
- How do I deal with recognition?
- How do I ensure the right amount of autonomy?
- How can I create greater meaning?

Authentic Adaptability:
- What is my organisational context?
- What are the situations that I am confronted with most often?
- How do I currently deal with those situations?
- What impact would I like to have in those situations?
- How can I adapt my style in an authentic manner to achieve that impact?

Your ambitions and your preferences

Before you start developing an action plan, it is a good idea to look again at the section on 'Authentic Adaptability' and, in particular, the chapters on 'Know who you are' and 'Know what you want'. The answers that you formulated to these questions will now be your guide for setting the right priorities in your action plan. 'Know what you want' will help you to invest in action points that are really important to you. Personal development demands time and effort, so you need to be well motivated before you start. 'Know who you are' will help you to build on your natural preferences and allow you to formulate your action points in a manner that matches the way you see yourself. This will result in Authentic Adaptability, which means that you will be able to avoid adopting behaviour that does not suit you or with which you cannot agree. So start by making a list of the conclusions you reached for 'Know what you want' and 'Know who you are'. Once you have done this, you are ready to start drawing up your action plan.

The power of habit

We are what we repeatedly do. Excellence then is a habit. Will Durant

Before we start with the two guiding principles of The Leadership Connection — Positive Connection and Authentic Adaptability — I would like to look briefly at the power of habit. This is where my expertise as an IT specialist is useful, because our habits are a kind of programming for the human brain. Our habits determine, often unconsciously, the way we react to situations. Neurobiologists, cognitive psychologists and other scientists estimate that between 40 and 95 % of what we think, say and do is a matter of habit. We react in the way that we are programmed to react. Some of these habits are inborn; others are learnt as we progress through life, usually because they have been beneficial in the past, either to ourselves or to our parents and forefathers. Often, however, this is no longer the case. It was a good idea to spread butter or lard on your bread back in the days when people had to work in the wind and the cold out on the fields, but nowadays, when we spend most of our time sitting behind a computer, it only gets you fat!

Perhaps you think that habit is only something that applies to routine tasks, like cleaning your teeth, crossing the road or getting dressed each morning. But nothing could be further from the truth. Many of the tasks that you think you have thought through carefully are also routine. The way you write your mails, the way you plan your work, the way you conduct research: these are all examples of things that you do according to a fixed pattern. This applies equally to the way you deal and work with others. For example, if someone makes a comment that you do not agree with, you will have your own 'standard' way to react: aggressive, compliant, silent, etc. To a large extent, your interactions with others are determined by habit. In turn, these habits are determined, at least in part, by your preferences, values and beliefs, as discussed in the section on Authentic Adaptability.

Each habit has three stages: a trigger, a routine and a result. For example, your child tries to cross the road when the light is red (reason), which causes you to grab hold of his/her hand (routine), thereby ensuring that the child, with or without tears, remains standing on the pavement (result). Similarly, you start each presentation (reason) by explaining the preparatory work you have done (routine), only to conclude that after ten minutes your public is no longer listening (result). If you want to change aspects of behaviour because you are not happy with the effect they achieve or fail to achieve, you need to devote attention to these three steps: reason, routine and result.

Is this actually possible? Is it not the case that our habits are so strongly programmed that all we can do is follow them? Is it realistic to expect that we can re-programme them ourselves? Yes, it is! Two of the best books on this theme are Carol Dweck's *Mindset – Changing the way you think to fulfil your potential* and Charles Duhigg's *The Power of Habit*. Together with various other experts and scientists, they have shown us that you can consciously intervene in the space between 'reason' and 'routine'. If a particular reason calls up all different kinds of thoughts and feelings that you can sense are leading you towards a pre-programmed reaction, you have the option to intervene at that point, so that you can react in a different way. In fact, in this context, 'react' is probably not the right word to use. Instead, you decide to 'act' consciously in a way that is different from what your unconscious programming had intended.

Intervening in this manner between reason and routine is easier said than done. To some extent, it depends on the nature of the reason and the routine. It is easier to learn to drink an extra glass of water whenever you drink a cup of coffee than it is to learn how to stop smoking during a period when you are under stress. Moreover, you cannot learn how to do these things by reading about them in a book or listening to a lecture. In other words, just flicking through the pages of this section of the book will not (sadly) be enough. Practice, practice and more practice is the only way to succeed. Reprogramming old habits into new ones demands action. Whenever you are confronted with a reason for doing something that you want to change, you must consciously implement a new routine. And not just once: you need to repeat the same process many times. Although books will often guarantee you success after 21 days, or 60 days or n-days, in practice it is impossible to predict exactly when the new habit will become established as 'standard'. A lot depends on the level of your motivation to achieve a different result by changing your routine, although the degree of difficulty of the new routine also plays a role. If you know that you need eight hours of sleep each night to avoid having a migraine the next day, you will probably be more motivated to do this than if you want to cut down on eating your favourite crisps, simply because your cholesterol is a little on the high side.

Learning new habits starts with looking at the advantages and disadvantages of the current result. Imagine that you regularly interrupt others at the point when you think that their explanation is too long. What is the most important advantage you gain? The time that you save? How important is the time it saves? And what is the most important disadvantage? Perhaps that the person you are talking with no longer feels respected? Or will no longer be inclined to listen to you? Or will no longer want to work with you? Without having a strong motive, you will not succeed in changing your routines. If you let others speak until they have finished, perhaps these others will be more willing to help you and perhaps this might save you even more time in the long run. This might be the strong motive you are looking for.

As soon as you are convinced of the advantages of your new routine, you need to be constantly on the look-out for the reason that triggers that routine. In which situations does this happen? Ask yourself where, when, what, who and how. In the above example, where you have a habit of interrupting people, you may come to the conclusion that you do it primarily during meetings towards the end of the day, in which people want to discuss subjects that are not on the agenda. If this is the case and once you know it, you do not need to be on the alert all day. Simply be on your guard whenever you have meetings at the end of the day with colleagues who have shown a tendency to disregard the agenda in the past. This will not only make your life easier, but will also allow you to ask others to help you in a more targeted way. They will know in which situations they also need to pay more attention, so that they can step in to support you, when necessary.

You are now convinced of the advantages of your new routine and you know when you need to apply it. The last question that needs to be answered is this: what does your new routine look like? Improvising on the spot is not usually a good idea. It is better to have a clear and well-considered plan. What will you do if a colleague raises a subject that is not on the agenda during a meeting at the end of the day? Are you going to listen to him and let him finish speaking? Or do you have a different strategy in mind? For example, you can agree to put the subject on the agenda for a following meeting. Or you can invite the person to discuss the subject with you in a private conversation. Or you can ask him to submit his comments in an e-mail, to which you can then react. Which of these possible new routines will give you the best result? That is the key question you need to ask.

Bringing out the best in yourself and in others by building Positive Connections and investing in Authentic Adaptability requires you to look at all your habits in this way. Do they contribute towards the objectives you want to attain? This is the essence of the personal development that I hope to realise with The Leadership Connection. You must become aware of the impact of your behaviour on yourself and on others. In this way, you will be able, when desired and where necessary, to adapt your behaviour in order to achieve better results. Results that will benefit you, your colleagues and the organisation.

Emotions as the starting point

> No matter the *feelings*.
> You can transform
> the energy of your *emotions*
> into your power. Matthew Donnelly

When talking about leadership development, reference is traditionally made to a personal development plan (PDP) or a personal action plan (PAP). In this kind of plan, you take as your starting point the new mental perspective relating to the attitudes, knowledge and skills that you wish to develop. This usually involves looking at your less well developed competencies, with the aim of bringing them to a higher level through training, coaching and other development techniques. In reality, however, these plans (regrettably) seldom achieve their objectives. All too often they are confined to participation in a few extra training courses, the content of which is only marginally applied practice. As a result, the power of habit means that you easily fall back into your old routines.

In The Leadership Connection you approach development in a different way. You start with your emotions. When it comes to motivation, emotions are much stronger than thoughts. As we saw in the above section about the learning of new habits, having the right motivation to change is an important factor for success. In the professional jargon, this is often referred to as 'learning tension': you need to feel a certain degree of intensity, if you want to learn.

In the first instance, the emotions that you take as your starting point should be positive emotions: what do you find meaningful, what makes you happy and excited? You can achieve these positive emotions by building on your talents. In the active implementation of The Leadership Connection, an important first step is therefore to search for ways that you can use your talents in more and different situations. Positive energy is the motor that will allow you to bring out the best in yourself more frequently. At the same time, you also need to consider your negative emotions: what frustrates you, what makes you feel concerned, what do you regret? Where are you sufficiently dissatisfied to feel motivated to change things for the better? This still means that you will focus on your talents, but you need to search for points of connection to which you can attach those talents. As we saw in the section 'Guiding principle 2 – Authentic Adaptability', you need to adjust your behaviour to match the context, if you wish to have the desired impact.

In other words, both kinds of emotions – the positive and the negative – will lead you to concentrate on your talents. Unlike the classic personal action plan, The Leadership Connection does not attempt to convert your weak points into talents at all costs. This latter approach has little chance of success and uses up huge amounts of your energy. In other words, energy that is no longer available for investment in your real talents. However, you do need to devote attention to possible pitfalls. Pitfalls often arise if you exaggerate or overplay your talents, so that they actually become weaknesses. If you are not careful, directive can become dictatorial, thorough can become perfectionist, creativity can become chaos, empathy can become failing to stand up for yourself, and so on.

There are many different models for mapping your emotions. In The Leadership Connection I work with the four basic emotions: happiness, sadness, anger and fear. These emotions are frequently given different names, often depending on their intensity. For example, 'satisfied' can be interpreted as 'a little bit happy', just as 'ecstatic' generally means 'very, very happy'. The emotional value and intensity of these words is something personal: 'satisfied' and 'ecstatic' probably mean something different for you than they do for me. Below, I have given some of the most common alternative names for each of the four basic emotions, ordered from least intense to most intense. Please feel free to add your own names and to vary the order of intensity.

- Happy
  - Relieved
  - Carefree
  - Satisfied
  - Cheerful
  - Energetic
  - Enthusiastic
  - Proud
  - Grateful
  - Delighted
  - Ecstatic
  - your choices...

- Sad
  - Misunderstood
  - Disappointed
  - Regretful
  - Joyless
  - Sombre
  - Unappreciated
  - Hurt
  - Rejected
  - Miserable
  - Despondent
  - your choices...

- Angry
  - Dissatisfied
  - Frustrated
  - Irritated
  - Indignant
  - Annoyed
  - Bitter
  - Rebellious
  - Furious
  - Enraged
  - Hostile
  - your choices...

- Afraid
  - Uncertain
  - Distrustful
  - Concerned
  - Worried
  - Tense
  - Inhibited
  - Nervous
  - Anxious
  - Threatened
  - Panic-stricken
  - your choices...

Situations as triggers

It is not the **strongest** of the species that ***survives***, nor the most **intelligent**, but the one most adaptable to ***change***. Charles Darwin

When drawing up and implementing your personal action plan, you not only need to take account of your emotions, but also of the various situations in which you have found yourself in the past. Situations in which you had an impact that made you and others 'happy', but also situations in which you felt so 'angry', 'sad' or 'afraid' that you desperately wanted to change something. In this way, you can discover in which situations your approach was successful and in which situations it failed. If you were successful in certain situations, see how you can apply that approach in other situations. If you failed in certain situations, see how you can apply your talents in a different way next time, so that you can achieve a better result. Put simply, you need to learn from your past. To make this possible, I use the STAR model (S – Situation, T – Task, A – Action, R – Result).

Situation = What was the situation?
- Who was involved?
- What was the nature of the activity?
- What was the timing?
- What was the culture/atmosphere?
- What were the circumstances?
- What were the other contextual factors?

Task = what was/were your task(s)?

- Listening
- Informing
- Implementing
- Deciding
- Following up
- Giving/receiving advice
- Consulting
- Observing
- I did not have a formal task.
- Other

Action = what action did you take?

- What did you ask – from whom – in what manner?
- What did you say – to whom – in what manner?
- What did you do – with whom – in what manner?
- What did you NOT ask, say or do?
- Other

Result = what was the result?

- Think about 'hard' results; for example:
  - a plan was drawn up
  - a project was implemented
  - a decision was taken
  - results were checked
  - …
- Think about 'soft' results; for example:
  - the team atmosphere was improved
  - a conflict was resolved
  - motivation improved
  - engagement was created
  - …
- How did you feel?
- How did the other people who were involved feel?

The STAR technique is often used during recruitment interviews. Candidate employees are first questioned about their strongest competencies. The interviewer then asks the candidate to give an example of where he has used those competencies, posing the questions of the STAR technique to extract more information: 'What was the situation?', 'What was your task?', 'What did you do?' and 'What was the result?'. Sometimes, there follows a final question: 'What would you do differently?'

For The Leadership Connection action plan, you need to work in the opposite direction. Start first with the final step of the STAR plan: the Result. In particular, identify which 'happy', 'sad', 'angry' or 'fearful' emotions the result generated in you and in others. How 'happy' (or not) were you with this result? How 'happy' (or not) were the others? In addition, it is also necessary to look at the nature of the result, making a distinction between 'hard' outcomes, like 'the right machine was installed', and 'soft' outcomes, like 'the atmosphere in the team improved'. In this way, you get a complete evaluation of all aspects of the result.

Once you know this, you can investigate which Actions led to these results. Focus in particular on your own actions. What did you do and how did this contribute to the outcome? Which talents did you use and how did you use them? What were the crucial factors for success? Where and when did you leave your comfort zone? How did you work together with others? You can learn a lot from the answers to these questions. What did you do that had a positive impact on the result? Perhaps these are actions that you can use more often when carrying out tasks in other situations. In which case, you have your first action point! What did you do that had a negative impact on the result? Perhaps these are actions that you need to replace with different actions in future. Or did you fall foul of one of the pitfalls? Did you push the application of your talents too far? If so, it may be a good idea to try less hard or to abandon imposing your favourite way of working. Alternatively, you can try to use a different action that is better suited to the task and/or situation, in the hope of achieving a better result. Whichever way you look at it, these are all potentially interesting action points.

After analysing your actions, it is time to move on to your task(s) and situation(s). Your tasks can indicate what triggers you to take particular actions. If, for example, you are specifically given the task of finding a solution, you might be more inclined to take the initiative in meetings than if your task is simply to share your knowledge, without any more specific objective. Examining the situations in which you find yourself can also be revealing. Look at all aspects of the situation and decide which situational elements worked either for or against you. If you were 'happy' with the result, perhaps you can use the same action(s) in different situations. If you were less 'happy' or not 'happy' at all with the result, then you know that you will need to be on your guard when these tasks or situations occur again in the future. Avoid the mistake of falling into old habits and try to find a different approach in which your actions are better suited to the task and/or situation in question. This, again, should provide you with additional action points.

Figure 21 depicts the STAR approach in schematic form. In the following pages I will use this schedule to give examples of a Personal Action Plan for Authentic Adaptability. You can also use the schedule yourself, to learn from the past and to draw up your own plan for the future.

Learning from the past	Action in the future
‖ STEP 1 ‖ Result	**‖ STEP 5 ‖ Result**
• What did you feel? 'happy', 'angry', 'sad', 'afraid'	• What 'happy' feeling do you want to achieve as a result?
• What did others feel?	• What (hopefully) 'happy' feeling do you want to achieve for others as a result?
• What were the 'hard' and 'soft' results?	• What 'hard' and 'soft' results do you want to achieve?
‖ STEP 2 ‖ Action	**‖ STEP 6 ‖ Action**
• What did you ask, say and do, how and with whom?	If you were 'happy' with the result: Use successful past actions more often.
• What did you NOT ask, say and do, how and with whom?	If you were less/not 'happy' with the result: Avoid past pitfalls or Adapt your action so that it better suits the task and/or situation. = Action points!
‖ STEP 3 ‖ Task	**‖ STEP 7 ‖ Task**
• What was your task, objective or role?	If you were 'happy' with the result: Consider using the same action for other tasks. = Action points! If you were less/not 'happy' with the result: Be on your guard when you have to do this task again = try different **actions**.
‖ STEP 4 ‖ Situation	**‖ STEP 8 ‖ Situation**
• What was the situation?	If you were 'happy' with the result: Consider using the same action for other situations. = Action points!
◦ Who was involved?	
◦ What was the nature of the activity?	
◦ What was the timing?	
◦ What was the culture/atmosphere?	If you were less/not 'happy' with the result: Be on your guard when you find yourself in this situation again = try different **actions**.
◦ What were the circumstances?	

▶ Figure 21. **STAR: a summary of your action points**

For steps 6, 7 and 8 of this approach, also look again at the 'limiting beliefs' that we examined in the section on Authentic Adaptability. Check to see what prompts you to take or not to take certain actions: 'I can't', 'I must', etc. Try to build on the 'happy' feeling that you want to achieve as a way to convert your limiting beliefs into empowering beliefs.

Your action plan for Authentic Adaptability

> You cannot **teach** a *man* anything; you can only **help** him find it within *himself.* Galileo Galilei

The moment has now arrived to draw up your own action plan for Authentic Adaptability. You can do this generally, without focusing on one or more specific competencies. You simply take as your starting point situations that resulted in you feeling 'happy', 'angry', 'sad' or 'afraid'. In this way, you will discover for yourself which competencies are relevant for your action plan.

Alternatively, you can focus on specific competencies that you would like to improve. Think, for example, of giving presentations, working with others, delegating, etc. You need to go in search of situations where you have used these competencies, such as giving presentations to customers, collaborating with your IT colleagues or delegating to your project team. What were your emotions in these situations? What made you 'happy', 'angry', 'sad' or 'afraid'? These questions will allow you to explore how you can (and want to) use these competencies further or differently in the future.

As a result of this process, you will end up with three different kinds of action points:

> do more = building on your strengths;
>
> do less = avoiding your pitfalls;
>
> do differently = adapting your action to the task and/or situation.

Do more = building on your strengths

One way to make better use of your talents is to learn from past situations that resulted in a 'happy' emotion. By analysing your actions and your impact in those situations, you will be able to assess whether or not those same actions can also be used in other situations, involving other people and with a different timing, activity, setting, culture, atmosphere and circumstances. Take as your starting point a situation in which you had a successful impact. How and when can you use these actions in other situations to create a similar result in the future? Figure 22 is an example of what you need to do.

Learning from the past	Action in the future
‖ STEP 1 ‖ Result	**‖ STEP 5 ‖ Result**
• I was proud. • Others were relieved and satisfied. • We reached a consensus about the approach to our project.	▶ See left-hand column
‖ STEP 2 ‖ Action	**‖ STEP 6 ‖ Action**
• I allowed everyone to explain their own approach and let the other team members ask questions. • I listened carefully to all the proposals and showed understanding of each of them. • I led a discussion aimed at combining the best suggestions from the different approaches. • Using these ideas, we agreed on a single approach. • I double-checked to make sure that everyone felt able to support this approach.	▶ See left-hand column What could I do better/extra?: Have a short conversation with everyone in advance about their ideas on the approach = action point! Pay more attention to possible concerns about the final approach, so that the necessary action can be taken to alleviate those concerns = action point!
‖ STEP 3 ‖ Task	**‖ STEP 7 ‖ Task**
• To develop a concrete plan for the new team project that all our team members feel happy about.	▶ See left-hand column • I let my manager know that I would be happy to perform similar tasks in the future = action point! • I can also apply these same actions to mediate in disputes between colleagues = action point!
‖ STEP 4 ‖ Situation	**‖ STEP 8 ‖ Situation**

• I am a member of the IT team. A new project was assigned to our team, but to begin with there was a lot of disagreement about the best way for us to proceed. We needed to make a fast start on the project, which had a high degree of visibility within the organisation. My manager had asked me to discuss and agree with my colleagues on a proposed plan of action that we could all support.	• I can also use these skills during consultations with my internal / external customers = action point!
	  ◦ Who: my internal / external customers.
	  ◦ What: if they submit to me their request for a new IT system to me.
	  ◦ When: as soon as I know the individual wishes of my customers.
	  ◦ Culture / atmosphere: my customers can be demanding and are hard negotiators, because of the financial implications involved.

▶ Figure 22. **A STAR summary of action points – building on your strengths**

My action plan for Authentic Adaptability

My motivation:

- Pride in the result.
- Relieved and satisfied colleagues and customers.
- Developing an excellent plan of action.

Situations and tasks = triggers:

- I want to reach a consensus (about a plan of action) within our team.
- **NEW:** I want to reach a consensus (about a plan of approach) among my internal clients.
- **NEW:** I want to mediate in conflicts between colleagues.

Action points:

- **Extra:** Ask everyone individually in advance about his proposals for the approach.
- **Extra:** As soon as final agreement is reached, check to make sure that there are no remaining concerns within the group and, if necessary, see how I can best alleviate them.

From limiting to empowering belief:

Limiting belief

- I need to wait until my boss sets me a formal task before I can show initiative.

Empowering belief

- If there are some areas where I like to take the initiative, I should simply suggest it to my boss.

Coaching:

- I will let my colleague Audrey, who is always involved during my consultations, know of my intentions and ask her to give me feedback about my approach.

Do less = avoiding your pitfalls

Another way to make better use of your talents is to learn from situations that resulted in 'angry', 'sad' or 'fearful' emotions in you and others. By analysing your actions and impact in those situations, you can see what things you can do less or differently in similar situations in the future, so that you end up with a 'happy' result. In the table below we will look at what you can do less. This essentially means avoiding your pitfalls. For this, it will help to look back at the chapter on 'Self-insight' in the section on Authentic Adaptability. Figure 23 is an example of what you need to do.

Learning from the past	Action in the future
|| STEP 1 || Result • I was disappointed. • The customer was irritated and did not make a decision. • My boss was angry.	**|| STEP 5 || Result** • I am proud. • The customer is enthusiastic and signs the sales contract. • My boss is satisfied.
|| STEP 2 || Action • I made my pitch to the customer with great passion and conviction. • I explained our offer in great detail from beginning to end. • I wanted to convince the customer with rational arguments. • I gave the customer a deadline for making a decision.	**|| STEP 6 || Action** Pitfalls: I talked too much. I will ask more questions to see if the customer is still on board and if he still has concerns = action point! I went into too much detail. I will limit myself to the main points = action point! I was too rational. I will try to build up more trust = action point! I projected too much of the pressure I was feeling onto the customer. I will discuss with the customer how much time he needs to reach a decision = action point!
|| STEP 3 || Task • Making a sale: getting the customer to approve my final offer and sign the contract.	**|| STEP 7 || Task** ▶ Copy from the past • I can **also** use my new approach when following up on projects: if my colleagues and I are looking at how the project is developing, I will ask more questions, limit myself to the main points, build up trust and agree on deadlines together = action points!
|| STEP 4 || Situation • I had already visited the customer twice to discuss his needs. • My manager put me under pressure to close the deal immediately. • We need this contract to meet our monthly target figures. • The customer is someone who is known to hesitate and places great value on trust.	**|| STEP 8 || Situation** ▶ Copy from the past • If my boss puts me under pressure, I not only project this onto the customer, but also onto my colleagues. • I can **also** use my new approach in this kind of situation during internal discussions = action points!

▶ Figure 23. **A STAR summary of action points – avoiding your pitfalls**

My action plan for Authentic Adaptability

My motivation:
- Pride in the result.
- Enthusiastic customers and colleagues.
- A satisfied boss.
- More sales.
- Better project follow-up.

Situations and tasks = triggers:
- When I need to consult with customers and colleagues while under pressure from my boss to achieve quick results.

Action points:
- Regularly ask questions to check that everyone is still on board and if there are still any concerns.
- Limit myself to the main points.
- Try harder to build trust: ask how customers/colleagues feel about the situation and search for solutions together.
- Allow input from customers/colleagues to determine more realistic and more motivating deadlines.

From limiting to empowering beliefs:
Limiting belief
- I have to know everything and need to be very convincing to win the trust of others.

Empowering beliefs
- Others trust me because I listen to them and take account of their needs. Searching for solutions together is fine.

Coaching:
- I ask my colleague Jim to make clear to me when I am going too far with my rational arguments, and come across as dominant.

Do differently = adapting your actions to better suit your task and/or situation

A final way to make better use of your talents is to learn how to act in a different way from situations that resulted in 'angry', 'sad' or 'fearful' emotions in you and others. By analysing your actions and impact in those situations, you can see what things you can do differently in similar situations in the future, so that you end up with a 'happy' result. This essentially means adapting your actions to better suit the needs of your task and/or the situation. For this, it will help to look back at the chapter on 'Adapting to the context' in the section on Authentic Adaptability. Figure 24 is an example of what you need to do.

Learning from the past	Action in the future
‖ STEP 1 ‖ Result	**‖ STEP 5 ‖ Result**
• My two colleagues were irritated by the extra work caused by the complexity of the installation. • I was frustrated. • The customer was not satisfied. The installation took up much more room than was expected.	• I am satisfied. • The customer is enthusiastic. • My colleagues are satisfied. • The boiler is positioned in the best place, so that it is easy to install and leaves the customer the maximum available space.
‖ STEP 2 ‖ Action	**‖ STEP 6 ‖ Action**
• Unload everything from the delivery van and get it ready for installation. • Install and test the boiler. • Tidy up the installation site and load all the equipment back into the van. **What I did NOT do:** Make clear my opinion about the best place to install the boiler. During his consultations with the customer, my colleague (who usually co-ordinates these matters) had decided on the 'best' place to install the boiler. Later, I had noticed that this was not the best place, because it would involve the use of unnecessary piping and result in difficult connections, which would leave the customer less space.	• I will inform my colleague that I would like to be involved in the consultation with the customer about where the boiler should be installed. • I will decide on the best place in consultation with the customer and my installation colleagues. • During this consultation, I will point out to the customer and my colleagues the benefits that my vision will bring in terms of efficiency, speed and space (this our point of connection) = **action points!**
‖ STEP 3 ‖ Task	**‖ STEP 7 ‖ Task**
• Assist with the installation of a new boiler.	▶ Copy from the past
‖ STEP 4 ‖ Situation	**‖ STEP 8 ‖ Situation**
• Together with two colleagues, I worked on the installation of a new boiler in the customer's premises. • One of these colleagues attaches great importance to speed and efficiency. He usually organises the division of tasks, even though this is not one of his formal responsibilities.	▶ Copy from the past • I can **also** act as the person who decides in consultation with the customers and my colleagues the best position and configuration for other types of apparatus.

▶ Figure 24. **A STAR summary of action points – adapting your actions**

My action plan for Authentic Adaptability

My motivation:
- Pride in the result.
- A enthusiastic customer.
- Satisfied colleagues.
- Practical and more efficient installations.
- Lower costs resulting from less complex installations.

Situations and tasks = triggers:
- When I help colleagues with installations and when the positioning of apparatus is discussed with the customer.

Action points:
- I will inform my colleague that I would like to be involved in the consultation with the customer about where apparatus should be installed.
- I will decide what is the best place for the installation, in consultation with the customer and my installation colleagues.
- During this consultation, I will point out to the customer and my colleagues the benefits that my vision will bring in terms of efficiency, speed and space (this is our point of connection).

From limiting to empowering beliefs:

Limiting belief
- My colleague will be annoyed if I take part in the consultation with the customer.

Empowering belief
- My colleague will be happy if we can make the installation as efficient as possible.

Coaching:
- With each new assignment I will tell my colleagues that I would like to be involved in the discussions with the customer about installation. I will ask them to give me feedback about my ideas and to point out any things that I might have overlooked.

Conclusion

Your action plan for Authentic Adaptability now consists of a series of situations (= triggers) in which you want to apply new actions (= routines) that will make you and, hopefully, the colleagues with whom you work 'happy' with the result. You have set down on paper the various motivations that make you want to invest your time and effort in these actions and in the conversion of limiting beliefs into empowering beliefs. Finally, you have talked to the appropriate people in your work environment, asking them to give you the necessary push in the back, if you momentarily lose sight of your good intentions. You are now ready to put The Leadership Connection into action!

Your action plan for Positive Connection

> Your **example** is not the main thing in *influencing* others. It is the only thing. — Albert Schweitzer

The Leadership Connection in action means that, based on the self-insight you gained in the section on Authentic Adaptability, you will now search to find ways that you can bring out even more of the best in yourself and in others, via positive influencing. In the previous chapter, we have seen how Authentic Adaptability makes it possible for you to bring out the best in yourself in a manner that takes account of the desired results, the situation and the context. At the same time, this is also one of the most important ways to make a contribution to Positive Connection. Making full use of your talents gives others the confidence and trust they need to follow you. Performing well and in an exemplary manner creates respect.

But you can take building Positive Connection another stage further. You can do this by asking the question: who do I want to build Positive Connection with? You can approach your answer to this question from two different perspectives. The first is to ask yourself who in the organisation has the biggest impact on your work results and your job satisfaction. The second is to ask yourself about all the people with whom you collaborate to achieve results for the organisation. A good way to start drawing up an action plan for Positive Connection is to take a cross-section of these two 'target groups': the colleagues who have the biggest impact on your results and your job satisfaction and the colleagues you work with to achieve excellent results for the organisation.

Before you start the exercise below, it is also a good idea to look back at the section on Authentic Adaptability and, in particular, the paragraphs on 'The roles in your life'. This exercise will allow you to explore what you want to mean for everyone in your environment, including your colleagues. This will form a further good basis for deciding in which relationships you wish to invest and how you will do this.

Investing in good relationships in your work environment is always a good idea and always repays the effort. Various theories and studies have shown that connection is one of the most powerful motivators that we all share. We all like to be involved and to feel 'at home' in the organisation where we work. Positive Connection simply takes this a step further, in the sense that we positively influence each other in order to bring out the best in each other. Most of the elements in my vision of Positive Connection are reciprocal: think of the expressions of mutual trust, mutual respect and mutual recognition. This is one of the great things about investing in Positive Connection: you often get back as much as you give; you reap what you have sown. What better motivation do you need?!

In the following paragraphs we will look at how you can invest in Positive Connection. The most important success factors are time and attention, which are both scarce resources in the high-speed world in which we live. So think carefully about how, where, when and, above all, with whom you want to invest more, so that your action plan is a realistic one. It is better to have two or three initiatives or habits that you know you will be able to maintain than a long list of action points that are never implemented.

Do more = building on your strengths

Make a list of the people with whom you already have Positive Connection. Base this on your gut feeling: remember that emotions are more powerful than thoughts. Once again, you can approach this from two different perspectives. The first is to look at things from your own point of view. Who motivates or inspires you? Who gives your self-confidence a boost? Who do you look up to? In short, who gives you a happy feeling? The second is to look at things from the point of view of others. Who comes to you for advice? Who likes to work with you? Who values your feedback? Who looks up to you? In short, who do you give a 'happy' feeling to? Figure 25 is an example of what you need to do to create Positive Connection by building on your strengths.

Score the people on your list for each of the different elements of Positive Connection. Score from 5 (if the element is strongly present) to 1 (if the element is barely present). If an element is not applicable, write N/A in the appropriate column.

My colleague Peter

Positieve Connection element	Score: Me to Peter	Score: Peter to me
Trust		
Honesty and integrity	5	5
Being consistent	2	5
Taking account of the interests of others	5	4
Competence	4	4
Respect		
Respect for yourself	4	4
Respect for identity and diversity	4	4
Courtesy and humility	4	4
Listening to others and showing interest in their intentions	4	2
Recognition		
Knowing	4	4
Recognising	4	4
Appreciating	2	4
Autonomy		
The playing field and the rules	4	4
Control versus letting go	4	5
The safety net	4	5
Purpose		
The why	3	4
Translating the why	3	3

▶ Figure 25. **Scorecard summary for Positive Connection – building on your strengths**

On the basis of this analysis of your Positive Connection, there are once again two ways that you can approach the next stage, which involves drawing up a list of action points. First, you can identify the strongest elements in your existing connections and see how you might be able to apply them in other connections. Second, you can see how you can contribute to the further strengthening of the existing connections. To make your action points concrete, make use of the ten questions for reflection that were given for each element of Positive Connection earlier in the book.

The following action plan is an example of the first of these methods. Look at the elements with the highest scores in your existing relationship (with Peter) and assess why that score was high, based on the reflection questions. Then see if there are other relationships (for example, with William and Barbara) where you can use those same elements to make more positive connections.

Action plan for Positive Connection with William and Barbara

Elements that are strongly present in the working relationship with Peter (based on answers to the reflection questions):
- Honesty and integrity
  - ▸ I always give my honest opinion
  - ▸ I always tell things the way they are
  - ▸ I always admit my mistakes
- Taking account of the interests of others
  - ▸ I know what is important to him in his work
  - ▸ I always defend his interests, even when he is not present
  - ▸ I tell him honestly in instances when I am not able to defend his interests

My action plan for William:
- Honesty and integrity
  - ▸ I always give my honest opinion
  - ▸ I always tell things the way they are

My action plan for Barbara:
- Taking account of the interests of others
    - ▸ I always defend her interests, even when she is not present
    - ▸ I tell her honestly in instances when I am not able to defend her interests

The following action plan is an example of the second of the above mentioned methods: working to strengthen existing connections. Ask yourself which action points are most important for you, but also for the other person (in our example, Peter). For each action point, try to decide in which situations you will apply it. Remember that our actions are often a matter of habit, which are triggered in specific situations. This means that your action points will often contain the word 'if': I will do A **if** situation B arises.

Action plan for more Positive Connection with Peter

Elements on which I want to focus more fully:
- Being consistent
- Recognition

My action plan (based on the reflection questions):
- Being consistent: keeping Peter informed **more often** **if** my work has an influence on his work.
- Recognition: showing **more** appreciation for Peter **if** he offers to assist me during busy periods.

You can also check to see if the other person (Peter) can also contribute more towards a more positive relationship. You can either mention these things directly to him in conversation or else you can invest more in them yourself, in the hope that he will recognise this and reciprocate. Treat the other person like you expect to be treated yourself. In the above example, Peter does not show as much interest in your intentions (a score of 2) as you show in his (a score of 4). To improve this situation, you can explain to him explicitly that you have a need for him to show more interest in your intentions or, alternatively, you can show even more interest in his intentions (pushing your score up to a 5), with the idea that this will prompt him eventually to do the same for you. In this case, you could add the following action point to your action plan:

- Listening to others and showing interest in their intentions: <u>if</u> Peter has a different point of view to mine, be **more active** in questioning him about the reasons for the difference

Do less = avoiding your pitfalls

Make a list of the people with whom you would like to have a more Positive Connection. Base this on your gut feeling: remember that emotions are more powerful than thoughts. Once again, you can approach this from two different perspectives. The first is to look at things from your own point of view. Who would you like to get on with better? Who would you like to work with more/better? Who would you like more feedback from? In short, with whom would a better connection give you a 'happy' feeling? The second is to look at things from the point of view of others. Who would like to get on better with you? Who would like to work more/better with you? Who would like to get more feedback from you? In short, who would get a 'happy' feeling as a result of an improved connection with you?

There are two ways that you can search for the elements that will improve your Positive Connection: you can either eliminate the pitfalls that disrupt your relationships with others or you can invest more time and effort in the positive aspects of your relationships with others. Figure 26 is an example of what you need to do to create Positive Connection by avoiding your pitfalls.

Score the people on your list for each of the different elements of Positive Connection. Score from 5 (if the element is strongly present) to 1 (if the element is barely present). If an element is not applicable, write N/A in the appropriate column.

My colleague Tess:

Positive Connection element	Score: Me to Tess	Score: Tess to me
Trust		
Honesty and integrity	5	5
Being consistent	4	5
Taking account of the interests of others	5	2
Competence	4	4
Respect		
Respect for yourself	4	4
Respect for identity and diversity	5	4
Courtesy and humility	4	3
Listening to others and showing interest in their intentions	5	2
Recognition		
Knowing	4	4
Recognising	4	4
Appreciating	4	3
Autonomy		
The playing field and the rules	4	4
Control versus letting go	4	4
The safety net	2	5
Purpose		
The why	4	4
Translating the why	5	2

▶ Figure 26. **A scorecard summary for Positive Connection – avoiding your pitfalls**

On the basis of this analysis of your connection, you can go in search of possible pit-falls. This means that you will be looking for elements that are too strongly present in your relationship. These will usually be amongst the elements for which you gave a score of 5. To make your action points concrete, make use of the ten questions for reflection that were given for each element of Positive Connection earlier in the book.

Ask yourself which action points are most important for you, but also for the other person (in this example, Tess). For each action point, try to decide in which situations you will apply it. Remember that our actions are often a matter of habit, which are triggered in specific situations. This means that your action points will often contain the word 'if': I will do A **if** situation B arises.

Action plan for Positive Connection with Tess

Elements (pitfalls) that I want to restore to normal in this connection:
- Taking account of the interests of others
    - ▸ I lean **too much** in favour of Tess and always follow her opinion.
- Translating the why
    - ▸ If I have to work together with Tess on activities that in my opinion have **too little** added value, I quickly lose interest.

My action plan (based on answers to the reflection questions):
- Taking account of the interests of others
    - ▸ **If** we have different opinions on a subject, I will share my opinion with Tess and together we will investigate how the best elements of both opinions can be combined.
- Translating the why
    - ▸ **If** Tess asks me to work on activities that are important to her, I will see if or how I can help her in the most effective way.

You can also check to see if the other person has pitfalls of his/her own. You can either mention these things directly in conversation. Or else you can adjust your own behaviour, so that the other person can avoid the pitfall.

In the above example, Tess often comes to your aid when things are going wrong. As a result, she is too much of a safety net for you (a score of 5). She makes your life too easy, so that you will never improve. You can either discuss this with Tess, telling her that you need more space to solve problems for yourself, even if you make mistakes, or else you can consciously make less of use of Tess as a safety net and solve your problems independently. In this case, you could add the following action point to your action plan:

- Safety net: **If** I make a mistake, I will not go immediately to Tess to ask for advice, but will first think of a solution myself, before proposing it to Tess and then carrying it out unaided.

Do differently = investing more and better in Positive Connection

As with the pitfalls, make a list of the people with whom you would like to have a more Positive Connection. Search for ways that will allow you to invest more and differently in your relationships with these people. Figure 27 is an example of what you need to do to develop a better Positive Connection by greater and more varied investment in others.

Score the people on your list for each of the different elements of Positive Connection. Score from 5 (if the element is strongly present) to 1 (if the element is barely present). If an element is not applicable, write N/A in the appropriate column.

My colleague Sam:

Positive Connection element	Score: Me to Sam	Score: Sam to me
Trust		
Honesty and integrity	3	5
Being consistent	4	5
Taking account of the interests of others	4	4
Competence	4	4
Respect		
Respect for yourself	5	5
Respect for identity and diversity	4	2
Courtesy and humility	4	3
Listening to others and showing interest in their intentions	2	4
Recognition		
Knowing	4	4
Recognising	4	4
Appreciating	1	2
Autonomy		
The playing field and the rules	4	4
Control versus letting go	3	4
The safety net	5	5
Purpose		
The why	5	4
Translating the why	5	4

▶ Figure 27. **A scorecard summary for Positive Connection – investing more and differently**

On the basis of this analysis of your connection, you can go in search of elements that are not sufficiently present in your relationship. These will usually be amongst the elements for which you gave a score of 1 or 2. To make your action points concrete, make use of the ten questions for reflection that were given for each element of Positive Connection earlier in the book.

Ask yourself which action points are most important for you, but also for the other person (in this example, Sam). For each action point, try to decide in which situations you will apply it. Remember that our actions are often a matter of habit, which are triggered in specific situations. This means that your action points will often contain the word 'if': I will do A **if** situation B arises.

Action plan for Positive Connection with Sam

Elements in which I want to invest more heavily or in a different way in this connection:

- Listening to others and showing interest in their intentions
    - ▸ If he comes to me with a proposal, I seldom ask Sam about his intentions.
- Appreciating
    - ▸ I make too little time to show appreciation for Sam's exceptional contributions.

My action plan (based on answers to the reflection questions):

- Listening to others and showing interest in their intentions
    - ▸ Even **if** I am wholly convinced that my own opinion is right, I will still search to find out more about the intentions behind Sam's proposals.
- Appreciating
    - ▸ **If** Sam makes an exceptional contribution, I will compliment him on the elements in his approach that I found to be original and creative.

You can also check to see if the other person can invest more or differently in your Positive Connection. You can either mention these things directly in conversation. Or else you can adjust your own behaviour, in the hope that your good example will inspire the other person to do the same.

In the above example, it is clear that Sam also gives you too little appreciation (a score of 2) and too little respect for your identity (again a score of 2). To improve this situation, you can explain to him explicitly that you have a need for him to show more appreciation and respect for your identity or, alternatively, you can show more appreciation for his efforts (which you were planning to do, anyway) and more respect for his identity, with the idea that this will prompt him eventually to do the same for you. In this case, you could add the following action point to your action plan:

- Respect for identity and diversity: **If** Sam attaches value to something that for me is less important, I will still take account of the value that it has for Sam.

Conclusion

In the previous section, I made a distinction between doing more, doing less and doing differently. In reality, most connections in a work environment will contain all three elements. In every working relationship you will find things that you want to do more often, less often or better. Your action plan for Positive Connection will consist of a series of actions (= routines), often linked to situations (= triggers) that will allow you to achieve improved Positive Connections with a number of people who are important to you in your work environment (= results). As a result, you will have an action plan that is truly personal for each of them. The time has now come for putting all those plans into practice!

Conclusion

Success is a journey, not a *destination* Arthur Ashe

You now have a situational action plan for both Positive Connection and Authentic Adaptability. You have mapped out the situations in which you want to adjust your approach by doing more, doing less or doing differently. If you find yourself in one of these situations, you know that you need to be on your guard to prevent yourself from falling back automatically into bad habits. Instead, you need to consciously implement your new behaviour. It takes concentration and mindfulness to be aware of this. Such situations often arise at the busiest and most difficult moments, when you are under great pressure. It is at these moments that your old habits will rear their ugly head. For this reason, it is useful to have one or two colleagues who are aware of your good intentions and can give you a friendly 'kick under the table' when necessary, to remind you to be faithful to your new approach.

Fortunately, you have taken emotions as the starting point for developing this new approach. This means that when it finally works, you will be rewarded with a 'happy' feeling. The more frequently you experience this 'happy' feeling, the easier it will become to transform your new behaviour into a new habit. A habit that you will not only apply in the situations you anticipated, but also in a growing number of other situations. Moreover, this 'happy' feeling is infectious and will inspire your colleagues to do the same, so that they can feel 'happy' as well.

Last but not least, a word of friendly warning. Do not be discouraged if you occasionally slip back into bad habits or if your new behaviour does not immediately produce the results you were hoping for. What you are asking of yourself is far from easy. New behaviour can often feel strange in the beginning and it takes courage to apply it fully. Be patient and don't be too hard on yourself if things sometimes fail to go as planned. Celebrate your successes and give yourself a pat on the back when things go well. That, too, is a sign of personal leadership.

Good luck! I wish you every success!

A WORD OF THANKS

I could never have written *Everyone Can Lead* without the help and support of many other people.

Thank you, participants in my workshops, my coachees, my customers and my colleagues of the past thirty years. Our encounters have provided the inspiration for this book.

Thank you, Mieke Smet, for giving me the chance at Janssen Pharmaceutica to exchange my career in information technology for a fascinating new challenge in the development of organisations and their employees.

Thank you, François van Vyve and Patrick van der Plancke, for giving me the chance at Galilei – Randstad RiseSmart to develop my ideas and plans as an independent consultant-coach.

Thank you, Wouter Adriaensen and Catherine Campo, for convincing me to write this book. Without your encouragement it would have remained nothing more than an idea.

Thank you, Niels Janssens, Lotte Demeyer, Tim Moriën and colleagues at Lannoo-Campus, for believing in me and my story, and for translating my vision on leadership into a book in a clear and attractive manner.

Thank you, Jo Beddeleem, my sparring partner of many years and my guide in my personal searches.

Thank you, Gretel Vlogaert, An Geypen and Evi Thonnon, for your willingness — in spite of your busy agendas — to make time to read my manuscripts and to provide feedback and encouragement. Together with everyone else at Randstad RiseSmart, you are fine colleagues and a pleasure to work with.

Thank you, Marc Van Harneveldt and the management of Randstad Group Belgium, for the many years of excellent collaboration and for your promotion and distribution of this book. I hope that this project will lead us to rewarding destinations.

Thank you, Frans van de Ven Snr. and Thomas van de Ven, for always being there as my *soul mates*. Both leaders in your own different ways, you continue to inspire me.

Thank you, Emma van de Ven and Margot van de Ven. You are two wonderful daughters and you give me so much joy and pleasure. I am unbelievably proud of who you are and I learn from you both every day, also in matters of leadership.

Thank you, An Van Overloop, my loving partner and the fantastic mother of our two daughters. Your vision on relationships has enriched the insights in my book, not least in finding the connection with Positive Connection. The path of my professional career was often restless and turbulent, as I constantly searched to find the right meaning in my work. Whenever the stress, frustration and worry became too much, you were always there to comfort and encourage me, with your endless patience, understanding and love. Words cannot express how grateful I am (and always will be) for your insights, your unconditional support and for all the wonderful moments we have shared together. I could not wish for a better partner!

Thank you,
Frans

ABOUT THE AUTHOR

Frans provides guidance to executive teams and their HR partners in the fields of leadership, talent management and organisational change. As a speaker, he shares his passion for – personal – leadership with audiences of many different kinds. As a coach, he primarily guides executive teams through major change processes. Frans works for a wide range of national and international clients, in both the public and private sectors. Amongst other things, he is also a guest lecturer at the Antwerp Management School and an executive coach for the Vlerick Business School. His approach is no-nonsense and pragmatic, characteristics that are clearly reflected in *Everyone Can Lead*.

Frans graduated from the University of Leuven in 1988 with a master's in mathematics and computer science. Until 1996 he worked as a project leader and manager for, amongst others, IBM/KU Leuven, Siemens and PwC. In 1996, he joined Johnson & Johnson, where he made the switch to the HR department in 1998 and was made responsible for talent and organisational development. In 2002 he graduated as an Executive Master in Human Resources from the Vlerick Business School. Since 2007, Frans has been working as an independent coach-advisor, in close collaboration with Randstad RiseSmart. As a coach, trainer and advisor, he has perfected his knowledge and skills through attendance at numerous courses, including those organised by De Baak, BlessingWhite and Ashridge Executive Education.

Frans van de Ven can be found online at:

www.fransvandeven.com
www.everyonecanlead.net
www.linkedin.com/in/fransvandeven
www.twitter.com/fransvandeven

Would you like to know more about *Everyone Can Lead* and how you can start to use it in practice?
Take a look at: www.everyonecanlead.net

BIBLIOGRAPHY

Ariely, D. (2012). *What makes us feel good about our work*. TedX.

Ben-Shahar, T. (2009). *Even Happier*. Mcgraw-Hill Education.

Ben-Shahar, T. (2010). *Being Happy*. Mcgraw-Hill Education.

Boyatzis, R., & Mckee, A. (2005). *Resonant leadership*. Harvard Business Review Press.

Brown, B. (2010). *The Gifts of Imperfection: Let Go of Who You Think You're Supposed to Be and Embrace Who You Are*. Hazelden.

Brown, B. (2015). *Daring Greatly: How the Courage to Be Vulnerable Transforms the Way We Live, Love, Parent, and Lead*. Avery Publishing Group.

Brown, B. (2018). *Dare to Lead*. Ebury Publishing.

Cashman, K. (2017). *Leadership from the Inside Out*. Berrett-Koehler.

Covey, S. (2020). *The 7 habits of highly effective people*. Simon & Schuster.

Csikszentmihalyi, M. (2008). *Flow: The Psychology of Optimal Experience*. Harper Collins.

Dean, J. (2013). *Making Habits, Breaking Habits*. Oneworld Publications.

Dewulf, L., Beschuyt, P., & Pronk, E. (2016). *Ik kies voor mijn talent*. LannooCampus.

Dowdy, J., & Van Reenen, J. (2014). *Why management matters for productivity*. McKinsey Quarterly.

Duhigg, C. (2013). *The Power of Habit*. Random House.

Dweck, C. (2017). *Mindset: Changing the way you think to fulfil your potential*. Little, Brown.

Frankl, V. (2011). *Man's Search for Meaning*. Ebury Publishing.

Gallup (2019). *Building a High-Development Culture Through Your Employee Engagement Strategy*. Gallup.

George, B., & Sims, P. (2015). *Discover Your True North*. John Wiley.

Goffee, R., & Jones, G. (2015).*Why Should Anyone Be Led by You? What It Takes to Be an Authentic Leader*. Harvard Business Review Press.

Gompers, P., & Kovvali, S. (2018). The Other Diversity Dividend. *Harvard Business Review*. Online: hbr.org/2018/07/the-other-diversity-dividend.

Harris, R. (2008). *The Happiness Trap*. Shambhala Publications.

Heider, J. (2013). *Tao of Leadership*. Green Dragon Books.

Hersey, P. (1992). *The Situational Leader*. Center for Leadership Studies.

Jaeger, B. (2005). *Making work work for the highly sensitive person*. Mcgraw-Hill Education.

Jung, C. G. (2016).*Psychological Types*. Taylor & Francis.

Laloux, F. (2016). *Reinventing organizations*. LannooCampus.

Leider, R. (2005). *The Power of Purpose: Creating Meaning in Your Life and Work*. Berrett-Koehler.

Loehr, J., & Schwartz, T. (2005). *The Power of Full Engagement: Managing Energy, Not Time, Is the Key to High Performance and Personal Renewal*. Simon & Schuster.

Lyubomirsky, S. (2008). *The How of Happiness*. Penguin Putnam.

Maex, E. (2006). *Mindfulness. In de maalstroom van je leven*. Lannoo.

Maslow, A. (2011). *Toward a Psychology of Being*. Wilder Publications.

Pink, D. (2011). *Drive: The Surprising Truth About What Motivates Us*. Penguin.

Redfield, J., & Adrienne, C. (1994). *The Celestine Prophecy: an adventure*. Transworld.

Rock, D., & Grant, H. (2016). Why Diverse Teams Are Smarter. *Harvard Business Review*. Online: hbr.org/2016/11/why-diverse-teams-are-smarter.

Ryan, R., & Deci, E. (2018). *Self Determination Theory*. Guilford Publications.

Seligman, M. (2017). *Authentic Happiness: Using the New Positive Psychology to Realize Your Potential for Lasting Fulfillment*. John Murray.

Sinek, S. (2011). *Start with Why*. Penguin Putnam.

Sinek, S. (2017). *Leaders eat last*. Penguin.

Snyder, M. (1984). *Public Appearances, Private Realities: The Psychology of Self-Monitoring*. W. H. Freeman.

Thacker, K. (2016). *The Art of Authenticity: Tools to Become an Authentic Leader and Your Best Self*. Wiley.

Ulrich, D. (1996). *Human Resource Champions*. Harvard Business Review Press.

Wood, J., & Nelson, B. (2017). *The Manager's Role in Employee Well-Being*. Gallup Workplace.

Yoshiko Seo, A. (2007). *Enso: Zen Circles of Enlightenment*. Weatherhill.